ROLLING THE DICE WITH YOUR LIFE!

"One Wrong Turn"

KENNETH WARD

Copyright © 2011 by Kenneth Ward
Los Angeles, California

All Rights Reserved
Printed and Bound in the United States of America

Published and Distributed by:
Professional Publishing House
1424 W. Manchester Ave., Suite B
Los Angeles, CA 90047
www.professionalpublishinghouse.com
Drrosie@aol.com
323-750-3592

Cover Design: Richard Ike
Formatting: Caldonia Joyce
         www.VisualBridgeDesigns.com

First Printing, March 2011
10 9 8 7 6 5 4 3 2 1
ISBN 978-0-9826704-7-7

Publisher's Note
All rights reserved. No part of this book may be reproduced in whole or in part, in any form or by any means, electronic or mechanical, including photocopying, recording or by any information storage and retrieval system, without permission in writing from the author. Address inquires to: Kenneth Ward kingdombiz190@yahoo.com.

Contents

1. Change — 11
2. A Hustler's Truth — 15
3. Where You Come From — 21
4. A Fork in the Road — 31
5. True Friends: Who's your Model? — 35
6. Accepting Responsibility — 49
7. Ditchin' and Death — 53
8. Teachers & Talkers — 61
9. Laws, Rules and Principles — 65
10. Finding a Good Woman/Man — 69
11. Hustlers & Gladiators — 83
12. Full Circle — 95
13 Finding the Truth — 101
14. My Truth — 105
15. Our Hope — 111

Dedications

This book is dedicated to my Mother, Gailey Ward, who has always been there for me regardless. She has always being so loving and supportive of all my endeavors. Mom, I love you so dearly. You have always been so loving and so giving. Mom, thank you.

To my father, Lee Ward, who reared my brother and me to be responsible in every aspect of our lives. We had to get up early in the morning. Dad would take no excuses. He made sure that we had balance. He always took us on trips and outings—it was always so much fun.

Thanks to my grandparents, Enoch and Irene Ward, for teaching us that getting an education is key.

I thank my grandmother, Janey Hall, for her agape love. She loved us all regardless, and supported us and was always there for us, and so was my grandfather, Mack Hall. He told and showed us that we could be somebody. He invested his money well, and was well off financially—he has gone home to be with the Lord.

To my bro, Julius Ward, and to my cousin, Anthony Anderson, our little brother, who lost his life to AIDS. We miss you both so much.

To my two daughters Rekenya and Kenisha my entire family and friends: To my uncle the late Rev. Fadell Beard, Sr., and to my cousin Rev. Fadell Beard, Jr. the late Pastor, E.V. Hill, Sr., Pastor, E. V. Hill Jr., Bishop Noel Jones, Pastor Marilyn Hickey, and Bishop Dennis Leonard.

To my parents in the ministry: Pastor Billy and Eltha Banks, Chris and Shelia Legrande, Larry and Debra Curry.

To Pastor Derek Anderson, Greg McDonald, Greg Moore, Louis and Romona Brown, my Sunday School Teachers, and my Grade School Teacher, Mrs. Smith, for believing in me and for teaching me that Jesus Christ is the way, the truth and the life.

Last but not least. Many thanks to my uncle, Matthew Hall, and to my cousin, Michael James, both of you have always been there for me in a time of need.

About The Author

Kenneth Ward, hails from a middle-class family. He was reared by both parents. From a baby, he and his brother, Julius, attended church with their parents. When Kenneth was 15 years of age, he and his brother made the choice to not attend church any more. This decision turned their lives and their world upside down.

Kenneth, after 15 years of being disassociated with the church—like the Prodigal Son, returned and gave his life back to God. He started attending church faithfully, and was later called to the ministry.

Kenneth, has served under the leadership of Bishop Noel Jones, Pastor Marilyn Hickey, Bishop Dennis Leonard, and has attended their school of ministry. He is currently in school, working on his bachelor degree in theology and Biblical studies.

Introduction

It has been 25 years since my brother died. My heart still hurts. He was 23 and I was 22. We grew up in Compton, California. But the Compton we knew was very different from the South Los Angeles pictured in the movies: "Boyz n the Hood", "Bring It On" and "Training Day". We knew and loved our parents. We were absolutely middle class. We attended church until we were 15. Then, we made bad choices. Now, I know better.

With all its violence (for a time, South Los Angeles had the highest rate of murder for black-on-black gang warfare), south Los Angeles remains highly polarized around the issue of geography—controlling territory. Crips, Bloods, Latino and Asian gangs all vie for dominance in trafficking drugs, arms, women and stolen goods. There's nothing special about this specific location on the map. Warring ghettos are the same all over the world. However, our existence is always about making choices. But for some of us, we aren't told about the importance of consequences.

We learned early to avoid gang membership. But we never considered "hustling" as a dance with the devil. As long as it offered the prospect of a life free from punching a time clock or hard labor, we were "down". (Accepting) Some see life only in terms of victims and predators. For them, the choice of affiliation is a simple one. Turning their backs on early morality lessons is easy. Others see those who willfully plunder as mad. No fair judgment can be made, however, without considering the full context. The title of this book refers to an observation it has taken me 25 years to understand. Living in South Los Angeles is, in some respects a gamble, like rolling dice.

The major difference in this locale as compared to Denver or Pittsburgh is the number and variety of temptations. In South Los Angeles temptation's pressure is frequent, almost unbearable. And, oddly enough, the wrong choices feel like the better option between the devil and the deep blue sea. In a place like Augusta Georgia or Billings Montana many people go years without rolling the proverbial dice, while others like Julius and I were forced to roll the dice daily.

The "fine messes" we got ourselves into often overwhelmed us. The consequences of being in the wrong place at the wrong moment, could literally mean life or death.

The night Julius died was my first real experience of throwing those dice. The choices that resulted are my lessons for you. It has been twenty-five years since my brother died, he was 23 and I was 22.

To the persons who killed my brother, Julius and Rick, my family, my friends and me, we have all forgiven you. However, our prayers are that you would turn your life over to the Lord Jesus Christ. God is the only one who can heal you and bring peace into your life. God loves you.

1. Change

I come from a long line of Bid-Whist-players. Playing this card game as family entertainment, I understand competition and gambling. Another game - played on street corners in locker rooms and Las Vegas casinos - resembles life in its purest form.

It's not a man's game - or, woman's game – instead a game like life, where risk has to be calculated. In Compton we call it, "Shootin' Craps" or "Rolling the Dice".

"Rolling the dice" is a familiar metaphor that speaks to taking chances where risk is involved. "Dice with death" means taking serious risks. "No dice!" is another way of saying "No!" or explaining that an action has failed.

"Shootin' Craps" is a dice game in which players bet on the outcome of the roll or a series of rolls of two dice. We would bet money against each other (street craps) or in a formal casino we would bet against the house "bank". I think you are familiar with the game.

Rolling the dice is like life in that if you want to see big returns, you have to take a risk. Yes, you may be scared (and you may lose more than you like), but the point is you try. And over time, all that trying may pay off. Rolling the dice, like a Chipotle burrito, is stuffed with possibilities. There's nothing like a swift roll and lightning crack at the start of a new game. Four, Snake eyes, and Box cars. The heart-quickening roll of the dice. That small snap and release of the dice is life in all its infinite possibilities.

We must champion Choice! Why? Because all change starts with choice! Whether it is our viewpoint, attitude, self esteem, or confidence level – the foundation stone is our first choice. And even if that choice is a wrong choice, we just have to make a "next" choice to correct it or halt the damage.

I remember feeling like I had it all; a 6-figure "hustle", "toys", a good woman, my parents and extended family, and all the other things that go along with my "fairy tale" life. Suddenly, my world came crashing down around me. I was only 21. My dreams were turned inside out; forcing me to make binary life choices. Yes or No! My hardest choice was learning to walk away. I believe we each have the power to make right choices. Do you?

How do you make changes?

I must change... for those to whom these words are true, they are never spoken louder than a whisper. These three words humiliate the speaker. That's who I was! These four words ring true for those who can testify about the letters c-h-a-n-g-e!

This is especially true for those of us who in a society that elevates knowledge and prides itself in being informed, become our own victims.

As at each crap shoot, we win some and we lose some. I found myself on a winning streak a few years ago. I felt I couldn't lose. As my winning streak kept building, so did my ego, and, I developed a swelled head. And then, just like that, the wins vanished and were replaced with loss after loss. The tide had turned.

We aren't perfect; we all make mistakes, say or do things we wish we could take back. Simply put, life is about being prepared for the pendulum swing, knowing that each extreme is temporary.

With every roll of the dice we calculate the risk and the odds. **We hope to win. With focus and clear thinking we still remain imperfect, we lose. There's always room for improvement. We must be humble enough to look for it and change.**

2. A Hustler's Truth

"Oh, how beautiful are our Emperor's new clothes! What a magnificent train. And how gracefully the scarf hangs!" In fact, no one would admit that he could not see these clothes which everyone seemed to think so beautiful for fear he would be called a simpleton or unfit for office.
"But the Emperor has nothing on at all!" said a little child.
"The child tells the truth," said the father.
And so it was that what the child said was whispered from one to another until all knew and they cried out altogether, **"BUT HE HAS NOTHING ON AT ALL!"**
The Emperor felt very silly, for he knew that the people were right, but he thought, "The procession has started and it must go on now!"

                                  ❧ Hans Christian Andersen

I HAVE ALWAYS ENJOYED THIS MORAL TALE OF TRUTH AND innocence. I have used it as a life-lesson as sacred as any proverb. Andersen delightfully presents the innocence of a child as being an essential human quality for telling the truth. If we can learn to openly express "our child within" then perhaps we all might have more integrity.

Another lesson results from the Emperor's denial of being caught buck-naked, and proceeding on as if nothing had happened. This reminds us of the "weapons of mass destruction" argument that has caused many to fear being, "called a simpleton or unfit for office."

Good books provide an indirect way to learn some of life's lessons, without paying the cost that experience so often requires. We get to discover our own truths, which can lead to positive changes and shortcuts. Saving time is the best return. It is better than the highest yielding return on any deposit in any investment account.

Reading tales of truth and original ideas can also have a curative effect on us. If we let them. It depends on our integrity. Our honesty; our courage. It depends on our ability to recognize and accept the truth.

This may seem like an odd question:

When our livelihood depends on hustling, do we have integrity?

"Please say, yes!" is at the heart of all selling. Whether said out loud or whispered as a prayer the sentiment and desired conclusion is always the same. Removing the moral question for a pause, is hustling an art or a science? Does it come with the genes or can it be learned? What do you think?

The answer matters. It is at the heart of all business, corporate or street corner.

Sooner than you think, the direct sales market will reach $100 billion dollars. Network marketing and party plan marketing are not going to disappear. Yoli, Park Lane, "Healthy Coffee", Mary Kay, Avon, Prepaid Legal and Tupperware all prove that the direct sales business model works. So how do you get your piece of that "hustle"? Through the art of teaching the common hustler how to sell. professionally!

I like watermelon. In fact, I love watermelon. I have eaten it as long as I can remember. I've tried it at room temperature, icy-cold, frozen in punch and most any way which you can think. I've tried all colors, all varieties and paired it with salt, lemon, lime, and even feta cheese. Imagine my surprise then when I was told the "proper" way to cut a watermelon. You see, from where I come, eating watermelon is a completely private experience. This means only I can decide what is best for me, including how I eat or even slice my watermelon. Whether by chunk, half-moon, or even a wedge like the character Ben Quick in *Long Hot Summer*, it is a personal decision.

I have applied this as a metaphor to my life. The only Person I would ever listen to about my favorite salad-bar-staple would be its Creator.

But, enough about watermelons, for now, let's talk about something else of value. Have you ever made gumbo? If you do, use dry shrimp and not fresh shrimp. Believe it or not the flavor is more robust. I learned this from a homeless man. Why is this important?

It taught me that everybody knows at least one thing I don't. (Except about watermelons) Sometimes those things are valuable. When you own a soul-food restaurant named Big Mama's Kitchen, this seemingly small tidbit means a lot. Some tidbits are worth even more!

I have a tidbit that I think is an original thought. There are at least 27 differences between a salesman/woman and a hustler. What does that mean in the real world? Ka-Ching! Ka-Ching!

I have been trained among the greatest "sales forces" in the world. I don't mean Apple or IBM, though I know them, and I don't mean JP Morgan or Goldman Sachs, although I understand their business models as well. You can fill in the blank as to who you think that organization is. I learned more about sales there, in a field where value trumped price; than I ever have elsewhere, irregardless of the service or product.

What did I learn from that experience? People act according to their own needs, first. Then, people do business with people they like. But not because of what they say, instead it results from what they do and are. Yes, the best sermon or sales pitch only supports our individual example; and the real world truth of the organization we are privileged to represent. That is "Why?" people buy. Even if we are Crips or Bloods.

So what's the difference between a professional sales person and a hustler? Shelf life!

Next question…

Do people buy from sales people or from sales organizations? Maybe it's both. It depends on which the "buyer" respects more. You can be a so-so sales person working for a great organization; or you can represent a so-so organization but be a terrific "peddler".

In either case there are results. But, is it the "yes" you and your business partners desire? Even "hustlers" have to answer to somebody. There is still a chain of command, a pecking order.

Off the top-of-my-head, I can think of some very surface differences.

A salesperson respects his/her trade and approaches a customer or client with respect and a business framework/process. From venture capitalist to shoe shine entrepreneur, the winners have a plan and/or a "system". They don't approach their goals in a willy-nilly fashion, without a clue or a method for keeping score. It is not just "my" business but elevates to "The Business" which has a life of its own. And, like Shrek's onion, it has layers. The corporate vision is bigger than just one individual and the impact of winning or failing affects a network of people and systems. Moreover, the salesperson has a legacy or tradition of quality to up-hold.

Believe it or not, those words just as easily describe the successful hustler and his/her organization. I know, I'm speaking from experience

3. Where You Come From

A friend of mine tells a simple story. It may be typical of children born into poverty. He was so ashamed of his parent's house, when anybody would drive him home he would run to the house across the street as if it were his own. Then when they turned to leave he would sneak back across the street to his own house.

He never grasped, It doesn't matter where you come from. History reports on shepherds who became kings and those raised on welfare who become presidents.

A Bible proverb puts it this way: *"Better is a dish of vegetables where there is love than a manger-fed bull and hatred along with it"*—Proverbs 15:17. Does your happiness depend primarily on where you live, or how much money you have?

Jesse Livermore was known in the 20th century for making wise business decisions. Some described him as the most successful Wall Street stock trader of all time. As a result, he acquired great wealth. He lived in a 29-room mansion, and rode in a chauffeur-driven black Rolls-Royce.

Unfortunately, his life was filled with heartbreak. His marriages failed, he felt depression, and his sons were never close to him.. Finally, after losing much of his fortune, Mr. Livermore sat in a bar, ordered a drink, and wrote a farewell note to his wife.

Finishing the drink, he stepped into an empty coat room and took his own life. What can we learn from this? Look at our world, while some live in relative comfort, millions live as squatters, setting up shacks wherever they can. Others are not that fortunate; they live on the street, with perhaps only a piece of cardboard or plastic between them and the ground. Many of them eke out a living in whatever way they can—scavenging in garbage dumps, hauling heavy loads, or collecting recyclables in pushcarts.

Not only are inequalities between rich and poor found in developing nations but, as the World Bank states, "'pockets of poverty' are common in all countries." From Bangladesh to the United States, no matter how well-off some may be, there are those who struggle to have enough to eat or to have a roof over their head.

The New York Times quoted a 2001 U.S. Census Bureau report indicating that the gap between rich and poor in the United States has continued to grow. It said: "The most affluent fifth of the population received half of all household income last year … The poorest fifth received 3.5 percent." The situation is the same or worse in scores of other countries. A World Bank report showed that about 57 percent of the world's population live on less than $2 per day.

Have you read the Bible accounts of Jesus birth in the books of Matthew and Luke? Do you believe what is recorded there?

At the outset it helps to remember the purpose of these Biblical accounts. They are not biographies; they are Gospels. Of the four Gospel records, Matthew's and Luke's are the only two that tell of Jesus' birth and childhood. Their aim, however, is not to show how Jesus developed into the man he did. So Matthew and Luke did not draw on Jesus' childhood in order to explain what kind of man he became. Rather, they related incidents that suited the purpose of their Gospels.

And what was their purpose in writing them? The word "gospel" means "good news." Both men had the same message—that Jesus is the promised Messiah, or Christ; that he died for mankind's sins; and that he was resurrected to heaven. But the two writers had markedly different backgrounds and wrote for different audiences.

Matthew, a tax collector, shaped his account for a largely Jewish audience. Luke, a physician, wrote to the *"most excellent Theophilus"*—who possibly had some high position—and, by extension, to a broader audience of Jews and Gentiles (LUKE 1:1-3). Each writer selected incidents that were most relevant to and most likely to convince his particular audience.

Thus, Matthew's record stresses the Hebrew Scripture prophecies that were fulfilled in connection with Jesus. Luke, on the other hand, follows the more classic historical approach that his non-Jewish audience might have recognized.

Not surprisingly, their accounts differ. But the two do not, as critics claim, contradict each other. They complement each other, dovetailing nicely to form a more complete picture.

Shepherds—eyewitnesses, reported Jesus' humble beginning. The stable and manger where he was born are elements that even non-believers accept as true. Even those born in a taxicab or at a fire station today, don't consider their birth to be as humble as the Christ.

Moreover, about a month after Jesus' birth, Joseph and Mary presented him at the temple in obedience to the Mosaic Law. Their offering of *"a pair of turtledoves or two young pigeons"* (LUKE 2:22-24) confirmed their impoverished circumstance. The Mosaic Law required a ram, but it allowed for this less expensive offering in cases of poverty (LEVITICUS 12:1-8).

Get the picture? Look at whom God chose. Joseph and Mary did not have Job or Solomon's wealth. Instead, God chose a lowly, humble carpenter for the household in which his beloved, only-begotten Son would be raised.

As parents, this should serve as a clear truth that the best gift we can give our children—far better than material riches—is a home environment that puts love for God and each other first. As children, this teaches us that how we turn out is more important than where we started. Neither welfare, coming from a single-parent family, or living in the "projects" can predict how we will turn out.

How do you value life?

Is it Expendable and Disposable?

World War I is a classic example. Time and again during that terrible conflict, "the bodies of men were sacrificed to no purpose," says historian A.J.P. Taylor. In pursuit of prestige and glory, military leaders used soldiers as if they were worthless and totally expendable. In the battle for Verdun in France, there were over half a million casualties.

"There was no prize [of any strategic value] to be gained or lost," writes Taylor, "only men to be killed and glory to be won"

                                   ❧ First World War.

Such contempt for the value of life is still widespread. Scholar Kevin Bales points out that in recent times, a "population explosion [has] flooded the world's labor markets with millions of poor and vulnerable people." They face a lifelong struggle simply to survive in an oppressive commercial system in which "life becomes cheap." Those who exploit them, says Bales, treat them as little more than slaves—"completely disposable tools for making money"

                                   ❧ Disposable People.

But, if we value life, knowing that men are not disposable, what makes it valuable?

Most people would readily acknowledge that happiness depends more on factors like good health, a purpose in life, and fine relationships with others.

TRUE success is the achievement of the very best way of life, one that results from the application of God's standards and that harmonizes with his purpose for us. A person who leads such a life, the Bible says, will *"become like a tree planted by streams of water, that gives its own fruit in its season and the foliage of which does not wither, and everything he does will succeed"*—PSALM 1:3.

What about MONEY and WEALTH?

Many hopeful believers reflect the view of a number of religious groups that attribute material wealth to the blessing of God. If you do the right thing by God, they preach, he will empower you to gain the good things of this life and reward you afterward as well. The theology has wide appeal, and books promoting it are best sellers. But does this "prosperity theology" harmonize with the Bible?

To be sure, our Creator, whom the Bible calls *"the happy God,"* wants us to lead happy, successful lives (1 TIMOTHY 1:11; PSALM 1:1-3). Moreover, he blesses those who please him (PROVERBS 10:22). But for us today, is that blessing merely a form of material prosperity? The answer becomes clear when we understand where we are in the stream of time according to God's purpose.

A Time to Get Rich?

In the past, our God blessed some of his servants with material wealth, the patriarch Job and King Solomon being good examples of that (1 KINGS 10:23; JOB 42:12). Yet, many other God-fearing men had little, including John the Baptist and Jesus Christ (MARK 1:6; LUKE 9:58). The point? According to the Bible, God deals with his servants in harmony with his purpose for them at the time (ECCLESIASTES 3:1). How does that principle apply to us today?

Bible prophecy reveals that we are living in *"the conclusion of the system of things,"* or *"the last days"* of the present world. This era would be marked by warfare, disease, famines, earthquakes, and a breakdown in society—conditions that have plagued mankind on an unprecedented scale since the year 1914 (MATTHEW 24:3; 2 TIMOTHY 3:1-5; LUKE 21:10, 11; REVELATION 6:3-8). In short, this world, like the Titanic, is about to sink! In view of those facts, would it make sense for God to bless each of his servants with material riches, or would God have other priorities for us?

Jesus Christ compared our time with the days of Noah. Jesus said: *"As they were in those days before the flood, eating and* drinking, men marrying and women being given in marriage, until the day that Noah entered into the ark; and they took no note until the flood came and swept them all away, so the presence of the Son of man will be" (MATTHEW 24:37-39). Jesus also compared our days with the days of Lot. Lot's neighbors in Sodom and Gomorrah were "*eating, drinking, buying, selling, planting, and building.*" "*But on the day that Lot came out of Sodom it rained fire and sulphur from heaven and destroyed them all,*" Jesus said, adding: "*The same way it will be on that day when the Son of man is to be revealed*"—LUKE 17:28-30.

To be sure, there is nothing wrong with eating, drinking, marrying, buying, and selling. The danger lies in being so absorbed in those things that we take no note of the urgency of the times. So ask yourself, 'Would God be doing us a favor if he were to bless us with the very things that would fill our lives with distractions?'* On the contrary, he would be doing us a great disservice. That is not the way of the God of love 1 JOHN 4:8.

A TIME TO SAVE LIVES!

At this critical time in human history, God's people have an urgent work to do. Jesus said: "*This good news of the kingdom will be preached in all the inhabited earth for a witness to all the nations; and then the end will come*" (MATTHEW 24:14). True believers take those words very seriously. Hence, they encourage their neighbors to learn about that Kingdom and God's requirements for everlasting life—JOHN 17:3.

However, God does not expect his faithful servants to be ascetics. Rather, he wants them to be content with life's necessities so that they can focus on serving him (MATTHEW 6:33). He, in turn, will see that their material needs are filled. Says HEBREWS 13:5: "*Let your manner of life be free of the love of money, while you are content with the present things. For [God] has said: 'I will by no means leave you nor by any means forsake you.'"*

So-called prosperity theology is, in reality, distraction theology

If you became very rich tomorrow, what would you do? Slow down and enjoy life? Quit your job and spend more time with your family and friends? Take up a career that you really enjoy? Interestingly, many people who become rich do no such things. Instead, they devote the rest of their lives to making more money—either to pay off their new debts or just to get richer.

Some who have followed prosperity theology, however, are noting the damaging effect that materialism has had on their health, their family life, and the moral character of their children. Recently, books, articles, television programs, and videos have warned against overindulgence and have, instead, encouraged "voluntary simplicity." A number of sources point out that becoming absorbed in materialistic pursuits can make you sick—mentally, emotionally, and even physically.

Of course, concern about the dangers of materialism is not new. Almost 2,000 years ago, the Bible stated: *"Those who are determined to be rich fall into temptation and a snare and many senseless and hurtful desires, which plunge men into destruction and ruin. For the love of money is a root of all sorts of injurious things, and by reaching out for this love some have been led astray from the faith and have stabbed themselves all over with many pains"*—1 TIMOTHY 6:9, 10.

But is that true? Do those who live for money and material acquisitions really suffer for it? Or do they have it all—wealth, health, and happy families?

Look around you and the answer is obvious. Charlie Sheen, Lindsay Lohan, and Robert Downey, Jr. are prime examples.

As I look back at my own life, I remember the clear impact materialism had on Julius and me, as well as our peers. Movies like "The Mack and Superfly" became icons we wished to mimic. The cars we drove our manner of dress were images we saw on the big screen. We were not "original gangstas", no, we were not original at all. Not one of us!

Clearly the Crips were founded by teenagers. Their imitation of adult's thinking failed miserably. But, their fights to defend the blue over the red, was no different than lives lost over the blue and the gray fought over 150 years ago. Same fight, same goal; power and glory!

4. A Fork in the Road

"*What profit a man to gain the world and lose his soul*" Matthew 16:26 "*There's a way that seem right to man but in the end there's destruction.*" Speed Racer, with all his excellence, just couldn't match up to his older brother, Racer X, no matter what he did. His older brother Racer X, was smarter faster, stronger, better. Speed Racer was the star of the show, he won all the races, he had all sponsors, promotions and endorsements. But no matter what he did, Racer X would literally kick his behind.

I can remember when I was 12 years old, my brother and I got into a brawl. With all my skills, let me tell you, my brother whipped my behind good. He beat me like Holyfield did Tyson, but I choose not to have a chocolate covered ear for desert. I chose not to do such a cowardly act; I took my beating like a man.

The next day, being a 12-year-old child, and liking to go out and play, I went across the street to my best friend's house. He would always have a porch full of people; he came from a big family with mostly girls. When he saw me, he asked, "What happened to your eyes?" I had two black eyes. I was ashamed and hurt, over what my older brother had done to me. I replied to my friend, "Julius did it." My friend didn't want to laugh, but beloved, some things are irresistible. He busted up laughing. I said, "Oh, what the heck!" I started laughing too. Even though my brother would get off in my rear, he wouldn't let anyone else do it. So when someone wanted to mess with me, my older brother would always take up for me very quickly with no hesitation.

My brother had a reputation for handling his business, and people knew not to run up against him! There are benefits in having a brother like that, if you take notes correctly, when you are being used as a sparing partner. Ali and Larry Holmes are a good example of such— iron sharpens iron. Ali had the upper hand, but one day the tables turned, Ali would put it on Holmes for years, but one day, Holmes had Ali backed into the corner.

My Brother's Death Changed My Life!

The day after my brother was killed, I decided I still wanted to get paid, but paid legally this time! I remembered what the Bible said about mind changing. *'Be ye transformed by the renewing of your mind!'* I said to the devil, "You have stolen and stolen from me, I'm ready to flip the script on you, devil. I've have lost to the world/streets my aunts, uncle, cousins, grandfather, and brother." The devil had stolen my family blind. The devil had robbed my family members of their youth, through the act of disobedience—enough was enough. The Bibles tells us that Satan comes to steal, kill and destroy; God comes that we might have life more abundantly.

The passion, the desire, and the thrill were gone from me. With the head honcho gone, it was just not the same. We tried to pick up and keep the business going, but it was just not there anymore. My brother Julius, he was the driving wheel, it was like trying to drive a car without a steering wheel. We knew it was over. The cover had been blown; there was a double murder, my brother, and Rick. There was now an ongoing investigation in progress. You don't have to be a rocket scientist to know when time is out! The investigators had the magnifying glass in places where the sun doesn't shine.

So, I got a job at World of Curls, a hair care manufacturing plant in Compton, California. I was working on the assembly line for minimum wages. My salary significantly dropped. I was not accustom to punching a time clock. I would work jobs a month, six months and then quit. I would quit because the money was so much less than what I was accustom to. I was used to making in one day what it took me one year to make working on those jobs God said to me, *"I will get rid of your enemies little by little"* EXODUS 23:30. My enemies were lust and greed.

5. True Friends: Who's your Model?

Examine your circle of friends, what do they look like? Do they look just like you or are they diverse? Birds of a feather flock together is a common saying, And, who you spend your time with is usually by choice. But, how do you find and maintain true friends? It takes effort.

It takes more than wishing, waiting, and reading books to have true friends. Learning to make friends is like learning to snowboard or play basketball. We can't learn either skill watching a training video. We have to get out and practice, even if it means falling down a few times or going to the hospital. Wisdom shows that the firmest relationships are deeply rooted in sharing common values.

Author Dennis Prager reports: "Flawless friends (i.e., those who never complain, are always loving, never have moods, are fixated on us, and never disappoint us) are known as pets."

What we are and how we turn out results from our environment and what we have inherited from our parents. Our religion and our politics are in many ways an accident of birth. If we are born into a Democratic or Republican household we are expected to maintain family loyalty and vote the same way. If we are raised as a Baptist or Catholic we are expected to maintain that alliance as well. Unfortunately, in politics and religion we are not given the unbiased permission from our parents to seek our own choices and draw our own conclusions.

From birth until we were 15 years of age my parents had a non-negotiable rule; Julius and I had to attend church services. We had to learn good from bad and right from wrong.

Our parents set the limits on who our companions were, and where we spent the majority of our time. But when we rebelled at 15, they abdicated their parental responsibilities and let us "nuts" run the asylum.

Why was their thinking "whack"?

Most adults understand the humor of Mark Twain's remark:

"When I was a boy of 14, my father was so ignorant I could hardly stand to have the old man around. But when I got to be 21, I was astonished at how much the old man had learned in seven years."

Our parents have a privilege and responsibility in helping us to choose friends wisely. As teens we think we are better equipped to make those choices than our parents but that thinking is flawed. When our parents exercise their "moral authority" based on sound ethical thinking, we young people win. When they doubt their moral authority and back away from setting limits, young people including Julius and I become like a ship without a rudder. Which means we drift according to the strongest current.

Dr. Ron Taffel, family therapist, writes that many parents "succumb to a series of media-hyped child-rearing fads" instead of actually parenting their children. Why?

"They don't know their own children well enough to relate directly to them." Moreover, they use the "children" from television sitcoms and media "parents" as models for their own parent/child interactions. Those TV models are designed to gain laughs, unfortunately, bad parenting or choosing bad friends is no laughing matter. The family relationships usually seen on screen are not real life, not real friendships, but the poisonous fruits of someone's imagination.

What can be done instead?. Parents must understand that children will look to their friends if they are not getting what they need at home. And what is that?

Again, according to Dr. Taffel, "They need what young people have always needed: nurture, appreciation, security, clarity in rules and expectations and a sense of belonging...The tragedy of our times is that most adolescents do not get these basic needs met by adults and do not feel truly 'at home' within their own families."

STREET CHOICES?

What happens when things go wrong for kids 14-17 years old?

Alex Alonso, *Los Angeles Street Gangs in Los Angeles from 1940 - 2000* and Donald Bakeer. *Crips: The Story of the L.A. Street Gang from 1972-1985*. Los Angeles: Precocious. Have reported the following:

"Raymond Washington, a 15 year-old student at Fremont High School started what would later become known as the Crips in 1969.

Washington got together a few other friends near his 78th Street home near Fremont High School. His initial intent was to continue the revolutionary ideology of the 1960s and to act as community leaders and to aggressively protect their local neighborhoods. The revolutionary vision did not endure and because of immaturity and a lack of leadership young Raymond Washington and his group never were able to apply their vision of neighborhood protection into a broader progressive strategy. They immediately were met with conflict by other neighborhoods, and slowly from 1969 to 1972 these neighborhood clashes led to murder.

The original Crip Gang members all had some common bonds. They either had an association through their High schools (Fremont, Locke, or Washington), Fred Shaw Home for Boys, Bob Simmon's Homes for Boys, or Detention Camps. In some cases all four. Most of the Original Gang--OGs were troubled youths who craved personal recognition. The newspaper article(s) that publicized the Crip gang's criminal activity, coupled with the attention (fear) they were receiving from their neighborhood became an attractive, volatile aphrodisiac. This recognition gave them a sense of real power, which they loved.

The Crip name, the Crip dress, and the Crip walk spread like fire throughout the Juvenile Justice System. A large number of troubled youth, who were in the juvenile detention system, wanted to be associated with this feared Crip image. Once these juveniles were released, they took this Crip identity back to their own individual neighborhoods, and formed their own Crip Gang. One problem developed though. The most hard core youth of each neighborhood wanted to be the leaders of their own neighborhoods. They wanted to have an alliance with other Crip gangs, but they definitely didn't want to take orders from any "outside" group, or person. The OGs continually tried to organize all the Crips into a one central command type of structure. That structure never materialized."

In Nature many animals instinctively and often ferociously protect their young from other dangerous predators. Mother lions are legendary for protecting their cubs from all perceived threats. Human predators victimizing the immature and innocent are the worst type. Should our human parents do less caring for us than wild beasts?

Robert Walker's Gangs Or Us, website describes a lost Raymond Washington and separates the romantic myths from the real truths:

Myth:

Raymond Washington's groups' original intent was to *"continue the revolutionary ideology of the 60's, and to act as community leaders and protectors of their local neighborhoods".*

*Raymond founded the organization in *"response to the increasing level of police harassment of the Black community"*.

Truth:

These statements are all romantic folklore with absolutely no substance. Raymond was just a troubled 15-year-old kid who hung around other troubled 14- and 15-year-old youths. Raymond had been kicked out of a number of schools, and had already been involved in the juvenile detention system. Raymond, at 15, did not have the maturity, or the vision to formulate these great ideological ideas and plans that some "social experts" espouse. Gregory Davis, who has also been identified as being another one of the original leaders was only 14 years old in 1969.

By the end of 1972 every area of the South Central Los Angeles felt the influence of a street gang. The Crips considered themselves "gangsters", or street thugs who were involved in every type of criminal activity. Their criminal activity was committed mostly in their own neighborhoods, e.g. burglaries, purse snatches, GTAs and narcotics. A number of anti-Crip gangs also simultaneously began forming at approximately the same rate as the Crip expansion. The first of these anti-Crip groups was the Piru Gang. This gang was located on Piru Street in the city of Compton. The OG Pirus came from an upper middle class neighborhood in Compton. Their original purpose of the Pirus for forming was only to keep the Crips from overrunning their own neighborhood. Note: This group did not fit the common societal mold of believing "only poor kids that have no future are drawn to gangs". A number of the OG Pirus even drove Fleetwood Cadillacs. Other anti-Crip gangs begin forming alliances with each other to combat the overwhelming Crip Gang influence."

Hence, the Bloods!

My Model

What do we learn from the "truth" about the Crips beginning? Two points:
1. Teenagers model themselves after whatever role models are elevated in their world.

2. The Proverb is true, *"He that is walking with wise persons will become wise, but he that is having dealings with the stupid ones will fare badly"* (PROVERBS 13:20).

It has been said that friendship doubles our joys and halves our sorrows. My best friend was my brother Julius. You may not understand how that could be, but it is factual. All the things that I couldn't do by natural talent or intellect, Julius did with gusto. When it came to dancing he was as smooth as James Brown and as elegant as Michael Jackson. When it came to sports, he excelled in both baseball and football. When it came to dealing with the ladies he was a merging of Denzel Washington and Christian Bale.

Julius was aware of my weaknesses as well as my strengths. And, he never used this knowledge against me. Instead, he permitted a balanced view of the total person that I was. He did not expect of me more than I was able to give. Can you imagine the gorilla his awareness removed from my back?

Mere acquaintances may demand perfection from us. Foolishly, they require us to have only good qualities. However, that's not possible for any of us humans. Not one of us has perfection to offer, and therefore we do not have the right to demand it of others. No, we hope there is a balance. Not one of us likes to feel our friends are too smart or too dumb. "Real" friends will accept us despite our imperfections and make allowances for us. Julius worked with what I had to offer, he accepted all of me. I learned from him to do that with those in my orbit. Finding a true friend and being a true friend is hard work.

Yes, to have real friends, we must open up to others—let them read us. Open communication and honesty are far more important to true friendship than having money, athletic ability, good looks or charm.

Dr. Alan McGinnis offers the key to lasting friendships this way:

"They have a certain transparency, allowing people to see what is in their hearts."

But, It takes time and courage to uncover the genuine person we are. And, our "potential" friends must believe we are worth the wait. Some folks have a natural and immediate affection for one another. However, it clearly takes time and shared experiences for mutual trust to grow. It takes more than the same uniform; whether you are a Crip, Blood, or USC Trojan.

When it comes to growing a lasting friendship this thought applies:

"Some people would like to take 9 women and create a baby in a month. But, it works out much better if you give one woman 9 months."

There seem to be natural affiliations among both young and old. Remember high school or college? Athletes, geeks, scholars and drama queens all provided clear separations. Some of those relationships continued through life, others were axed as soon as the graduation stage was crossed. The difference; "summer" friends versus "true" friends.

Unshakable and unbreakable are two words that describe true friends. We have examples everywhere. In the Bible we find pairings of individuals who from a surface view should not be close. David and Jonathan, Ruth and Naomi, Paul and Timothy are all prime examples.

What was the key to their friendships? Common values and the freedom to be themselves.

Have you ever gotten so nervous that your breathing is affected. You know. So nervous that you either hyperventilate or can't catch your breath at all. What a miserable feeling. This describes what happens when you cannot be yourself.

A true friend permits you to be yourself!

Therefore, just relax! Be yourself. Likewise, let others be themselves. Like Julius and me. Because to have a friend, you have to be a friend.

In 1978, Julius started working at Dodger Stadium. The Crips were rivals of the Bloods by then, and everyone in their teens or near-teens was being asked to affiliate, attach, or become a gang standard bearer. Colors—blue for Crips and the opposing red for Bloods could have an impact on your world that could mean life or death. Julius and I refused to join any gang, instead, Julius started hosting "Dice" games after work at the stadium.

So, what did this teach me about true friends? A lot.

Values

Have you read the scripture, "Don't be misled, bad association spoils useful habits"? Well, do you believe that thought? How can you test it?

As mentioned earlier, none of us is perfect. That means we will make mistakes and choose the wrong friends. We needn't feel bad about this, Jesus was perfect and yet he chose traitorous Judas. This so-called friend betrayed him in the garden of Gethsemane. This didn't stop Jesus from choosing others for friends.

The problem with Judas is clear. He and Jesus did not have the same values. Do you know what your friends' values are?

The answer to that question can literally mean life or death. When the Crips first formed they wanted everybody to dress alike. Robert Walker states:

"The original gang attire included an ear ring in the left ear, kaki pants, suspenders hanging down, brim type of hat, cane, and Stacy Adams, "Old man comforts" shoes. Gregory Davis, aka Batman, was the poster child for this OG Crip look. Note: Even then, not every Crip had this same look as some of the kids could not afford the clothes. The leather coat look was temporary and short lived at best. The leather coat was supposed to be stolen, and was a demonstration of strength and power as it had to be taken from someone else. This didn't last long either, as there were not enough leather coats available to be stolen. The cane, the suspenders hanging down, and the exaggerated "limp" look lasted the longest. The blue rag was also an early identifier of Crip association."

Gang leaders having identified a "uniform" moved towards expanding their numbers. Julius and I witnessed their methods, our age group and Compton home address made us the perfect targets. What Robert Walker describes we experienced:

"Gang leaders can build their organizations in several ways. First, they can claim turf, and intimidate any kids who live in the neighborhood—if you want protection from the gang, you have to join. Second, they can offer protection to people who are being persecuted elsewhere; victims of domestic abuse, for example, might be more likely to join up. Third, they can lure in susceptible kids on the basis of their reputation. Gang experts say that impressive physical stature can also help in recruiting: Tookie Williams, for example, had a large, muscular build.

Once a gang has some members and some turf, it can grow by starting offshoots. People in other neighborhoods, cities, or states can start their own branches of a successful gang (with which they may have little or no contact). Each of these subgroups—called "sets," or, among the Latin gangs, "clikas"—takes two names. The first refers to their specific locale, the second to the original gang, or "nation"—the 79th Street Crips, for example.

Smaller gangs may have no broader affiliation, or their affiliations might change so often as to be meaningless.

A gang can also grow by merging with other groups. **As the Crips spread** throughout the Los Angeles area in the early 1970s, their competitors—including the LA Brims and the Piru Street Boys—banded together to create the Bloods.

Gang offshoots can also turn up in prisons (along with brand-new prison gangs). In 1993, several different groups of Bloods on the East Coast merged at New York's Rikers Island jail to form the **United Blood Nation**. (Members went on to form eight new Blood sets to recruit from New York City streets.) The **Latin Kings** followed a similar path: The gang originated on the streets of Chicago in the 1930s or 1940s, but the Almighty Latin King and Queen Nation was created in Connecticut and New York jails decades later."

We chose not to become Crips. And, we chose not to become Bloods. What makes these statements so amazing is that the groups who united to form the Bloods, came from the same middle class neighborhoods with the same middle class values with which Julius and I were raised. We liked the same Cadillacs and Fatburgers.

I cannot brag, my corruption took a different form. Fortunately, unlike Julius or Tookie Williams or Raymond Washington I lived to find my redemption.

Many of us select friends merely on the basis of whether we "are down" or not—how we feel when we are around them. Or, if we are selfish, we just think about what they can do for us. But either reason makes a weak foundation upon which to build a long-term relationship.

How can you know whether a person has good values? To recognize them, you must have good values yourself.

Sunday School taught us wisdom's higher authority, the Bible. The standards and principles set forth in this highest authority are the measure of good values. It can give practical and successful answers.

By the time I was 16, I forgot most of the chapters and verses, I couldn't find God's name in the Bible if you paid me. But, even if I couldn't find the location, I didn't forget many of the truths.

There is one important truth I will never forget—the most fundamental one. Jesus taught that the key to success in every human relationship is principled love— **agape**. He taught the Golden Rule: *"Just as you want men to do to you, do the same way to them"* (LUKE 6:31). Clearly, the only way to have real friends is to be an unselfish, loyal friend yourself. In short, to have a friend, be a friend. To be successful, friendship must be more about giving than receiving.

So, let me share what I believe to be other true characteristics of valuable friends based on Bible principles:

1. Keith Ferrazi in **Whose Got Your Back,** describes "lifeline" relationships. In these, (3 to a customer), you have a friend who listens, supports and corrects. You can't get away with stupid. "Faithful are the wounds of a friend" (PROVERBS 27:6).

2. Our intimate associates must share our belief system. *"By iron, iron itself is sharpened. So one man sharpens the face of another"* (PROVERBS 27:17).

3. It is easy to talk the talk, but remember *"Out of the abundance of the heart the mouth speaks,"* said Jesus (MATTHEW 12:34).

To have true friendships, you don't necessarily have to look alike. You needn't be the same color, age or sex. Meditate on the fine relationships you already have. Try and see what you can do to strengthen your friendship with them? Loyal and loving friends are a uniquely precious treasure, and we should value them properly. Never take their loyalty or love for granted.

Please take note, true happiness—and true friendship—come from giving of yourself, your time, and your resources. The rewards are more than worth the effort and sacrifices involved.

I explained that for a season. I forgot my way. Having regained my balance I know this: The Bible shows that the best relationships are deeply rooted in love for God and his words of Truth.

6. Accepting Responsibility

PAUL SAID, *"WHEN I WAS A CHILD I DID CHILDISH THINGS, BUT now that I'm a man, I put away childish things."* We have to grow up and face up to our responsibilities whatever they are. It was once said that the thing you feared the most, is the very thing you were called to do. I can remember on many occasions the people I feared meeting and thought I didn't like, they ended up being one of the best persons I ever meet. Beloved fear is nothing but false evidence appearing real. Don't buy into that lie that the devil put in your head, telling you that it's not going to work out, trust God! Scriptures tells us *"If God be for us who can be against us"* ROMANS 8:28-31.

I can remember when, I had gotten fed up with having bad credit, and wanted to buy a home and enjoy the finer things in life. I would go to lenders and they would say "Sorry Mr. Ward, but we can't help you." So finally I hooked with a friend Ken Hall, who had his own mortgage company. He ran my credit looked at it, and said, to me "Kenny you really don't have that much to pay. Your debts are only about $2,800.00" I owed about ten different sources $40.00, $50.00 here, $100.00 there, $500.00, etc Ken Hall said, "Call theses people and negotiate with them, maybe you owe them $500.00 tell them you can give $200.00 right now to remove this off of your credit. Make sure you get a receipt." To stay motivated I started off with the smallest and work up to the largest. Scriptures tells us that a borrower is a slave to the lender.

It also tells us in, DEUTERONOMY 28, that *"God is going to make us the head and not the tail."* Once you pay your debt by law they have to show it as paid on your credit report. Does God want us to have bad credit? No, beloved. He does not. God says, I own the cattle on a thousand hills, The earth is His and the fullest there of. If our Father, God is not in debt, what makes you think He wants us to be in debt. Scriptures tells us that we are qualified to share in His inheritance. We are fellow citizens of the Kingdom of Heaven. You have not because you ask not. Stretch out your faith and believe God for whatever it is that you believe. Hook up with your prayer partner and literally shake the gates of hell. Tell the devil that you getting out my finances today. You are getting out of my life today, my family and friends life today. Therefore I tell you, " you ask for in prayer, believe that you have received it, and it will be yours" — MARK 11:24.

So I would do exactly as Ken Hall instructed, and little by little my credit score had began to improve. After removing all the negative items from my credit, then the day of triumph, I was approved by the lender. We can apply this to God's will for our lives. God wants to delete some things out of are lives so He can bless us. Beloved, God loves us but he can't bless no mess, we have to take the first steps and then Gods comes in, when you're in a relationship with your mate, do you do all the work to make the relationship work, if you do something wrong. So, why should God do all the work? He desires so much to have a relationship with us, but we have to put forth an effort.

Beloved, have a gratitude of praise and a thankful heart. The word tells us in all things give thanks, and rejoice and be exceedingly glad. God has His laws, rules, and principles already written, and He will not break them — DEUTERONOMY 28. It's up to us to walk in the blessings or the curses. He gives us free will and freedom of choice. Would you want to be in a relationship with someone that you always had to make do something? No! Neither does God. Taking responsibility for our actions can be something as little as flushing the toilet, and wiping the seat after your done. Why should the next person come and have to deal with that. *"If anyone wants to be first, he must be the very last and a servant of all"* — MARK 9:35.

Take the toilet paper or paper towel and use it on the handle and flush. Use it also to wipe the toilet seat, do the smart things that matter.

7. Ditchin' and Death

Why? Three letters which make a word that can change a world. Why not? Six letters that can change a way of thinking. I moved from 'Why?" to "Why not?" when I learned to meditate on free choice versus predestination.

Why was my brother Julius killed and I lived? Was it by choice or by accident? Was he just in the wrong place at the wrong time or was it more than that? I was there, yet I am alive. Why?

You may think, "It wasn't your time to go!" or " The Father called him and not you." But Julius' death was no accident. He didn't get hit by a runaway car or a falling rock. It was not an accident. It was premeditated murder resulting from a kidnapping, by a jealous enemy. Was that an act of God or a fruit of the Devil.

You may think that your life is predetermined. And, you may believe no matter what you do, the outcome is already set. You may agree with Omar Khayyam,

"The moving finger, having writ, moves on and not all your piety can lure it back to cancel half a line, nor all your tears wash out a word of it."

But was he right?

Moses told the Israelites at DEUTERONOMY 30:19-20.

"19 I do take the heavens and the earth as witnesses against YOU today, that I have put life and death before you, the blessing and the malediction; and you must choose life in order that you may keep alive, you and your offspring, 20 by loving your God, by listening to his voice and by sticking to him; for he is your life and the length of your days, that you may dwell upon the ground that God swore to your forefathers Abraham, Isaac and Jacob to give to them."

Were his words an eternal truth or just commentary for those Jews at that time? I have meditated on this question deeply. My conclusion—these words are a principle that will survive forever. We are free moral agents and we may choose our own life course!

At one time, I decided to name this book "Predestined." At that time it reflected my soured view of life and the choices before me. I believed that fate or destiny predetermined the man I would become. I believe differently today. Please consider the merits of my new-found logic.

Intellectuals compete on their views of humans. Moses words were given to the Jews. In the book An Intelligent Person's Guide to Judaism, Shmuley Boteach says, "Man is not an animal, and is therefore always in control of his own destiny."

But, evolutionist John Gray states, " Humans can no more be masters of their destiny than any other animal. Others throughout history have agreed with Gray, believing that supernatural forces controlled their destiny. The ancient Greeks and Romans both taught that man had a predetermined destiny. The Greeks were sure that the destiny of every person was decided by the Fates, goddesses who were in some ways more powerful than Zeus the king of the Greek Gods. These goddesses decided when a person would die as well as the quality of an individual's life.

Those today who believe in Kismet, or fate. propose that God has predetermined the outcome of all human actions and the time of each person's death. Asian Hindus and Buddhists believe in forms of reincarnation where a person's current life results from what he did in a past life. The good or evil he does in this life determines what he is like in the next life or "incarnation."

What do you believe? Are you ruled by fate?

Author Boteach, mentioned above, supports the Genesis view that man is made in God's image, at GENESIS 1:26, 27 we read:

"26 And God went on to say: "Let us make man in our image, according to our likeness, and let them have in subjection the fish of the sea and the flying creatures of the heavens and the domestic animals and all the earth and every moving animal that is moving upon the earth." 27 And God proceeded to create the man in his image, in God's image he created him; male and female he created them. 28 Further, God blessed them and God said to them: "Be fruitful and become many and fill the earth and subdue it, and have in subjection the fish of the sea and the flying creatures of the heavens and every living creature that is moving upon the earth."

Of course, this "likeness" means emotional, mental and spiritual image. This is what permits humans to show love, justice, kindness, forgiveness and a variety of other moral values.

A reasonable question for Mr. Gray is, "When was the last time you saw a lion forgive a zebra or an antelope?" Another fair question is, "Do both a praying man and a praying mantis seek the same God?"

If as evolutionists believe man is governed by the "survival of the fittest "doctrine, then no man could ever commit murder. From Gray's point of view, you would have to punish a cat for eating a mouse, if you punished a man for aggressive or deadly behavior.

Predestined? Again, what do you think? Has your destiny already been fixed by forces completely beyond your control? Or do you agree with Voltaire and Franklin Roosevelt?

Each player must accept the cards life deals him or her. But once they are in hand, he or she alone must decide how to play the cards in order to win the game.

Voltaire

> Men are not prisoners of Fate, but only prisoners of their own minds.
>
> ❧ Franklin Roosevelt

Is Free Will—Reasonable?

I conclude from Moses words in Genesis and Deuteronomy that God has given us the gift of free will, or freedom of choice. This makes us unique among his earthly creation and superior to animals. We can choose how we play the cards we are dealt.

Our God given freedom of choice, though, does not mean absolute freedom. It does not free us from God's physical and moral laws. Gravity a physical law and love a spiritual law are both principles that create a harmonious universe. These laws were set up for our good, and serious violations of either can lead to harm. Just think of what would happen if we chose to defy the law of gravity and jumped off the Eiffel Tower!

Freedom of choice, then, places upon us a heavy responsibility and makes us accountable for our actions. According to Galatians 6:7 and 8:

"7 Do not be misled: God is not one to be mocked. For whatever a man is sowing, this he will also reap; 8 because he who is sowing with a view to his flesh will reap corruption from his flesh, but he who is sowing with a view to the spirit will reap everlasting life from the spirit."

These verses would prove God to be unloving if he predetermined the course we would take and then severely punished us for our wrong actions! He does not do this, for *"God is love,"* and *"all his ways are justice."* (1 John 4:8; Deuteronomy 32:4) Having given us freedom of choice, he rewards our goodness and provides a means for forgiveness of our errors.

Therefore, good reasoning tells us It is unthinkable that God would give us freedom of choice and at the same time determine from the beginning who lives and who dies. Freedom of choice precludes predestination. Moreover, God's preaching either forgiveness or mercy would be a sham if our destiny was preordained.

Instead, again and again the Holy Scriptures clearly show that the choices we make and our individual actions determine our destiny.

Why do Bad Things Happen to Good People?

Many of us have been taught "the world, the flesh and the Devil" are the causes of our pain and suffering.

The world—includes all those using power and position to victimize others.

The flesh—reflects that all of us inherited sin and imperfection from our original parents.

The Devil—according to Scripture is a "manslayer" and "the Father of the Lie."

As a result of this trio we face the prospect of pain, suffering, and death. In addition, the Apostle Paul describes those in our day at 2 TIMOTHY 3:1-5 as:

> "1 But know this, that in the last days critical times hard to deal with will be here. 2 For men will be lovers of themselves, lovers of money, self-assuming, haughty, blasphemers, disobedient to parents, unthankful, disloyal, 3 having no natural affection, not open to any agreement, slanderers, without self-control, fierce, without love of goodness, 4 betrayers, headstrong, puffed up [with pride], lovers of pleasures rather than lovers of God, 5 having a form of godly devotion but proving false to its power; and from these turn away."

Clearly this description reads as current as the nightly evening news. Therefore, when we mix Paul's view of where we are in time and Solomon's statement of, *"time and unforeseen occurrence befall them all."*—ECCLESIASTES 9:11, we can only reach one conclusion. Good things happen to good people and bad things happen to good people. Sometimes we are the cause and other times we are in the wrong place at the wrong time.

But what about our own poor choices or poor timing?

No person on Earth had control over Hurricane Katrina or the earthquake in Haiti.

Good people were not exempt from accidental death caused during those natural disasters. However, the violence and crimes perpetrated during those natural disasters were man-caused.

My friend Norman died as a result of his own poor choice and poor timing. We were in drafting class together in high school. That warm Tuesday he and my cousin Andre decided to "ditch" or leave school for a few hours. He didn't ask me to go with him, or I might have gone, but I had a project to finish. On his way back to school, he was spotted by several Bloods. His blue colors identified him as an enemy Crip. He was shot in the forehead and was in comma for some days, after being in comma for some days he passed away,

The next time I saw Norman was in a casket. He was shot for choosing "ditchin'" over drafting class. And, Andre was shot in the arm. Fortunately he didn't pay for his bad timing with his life.

Understand choices?

I loved my brother Julius without reservation. Our times together were good, bad, and ugly. Our choices were also good, bad, and ugly. And, I miss him dearly.

Julius reminded me of a cartoon character—Racer X.

For the uninformed he is Speed Racer's older brother.

I saw myself as skilled as the younger brother, but speaking honestly, Julius had superior skills. Like Racer X, Julius was just better at whatever it was we did. Julius experienced "good" in so many ways.

During our "good" times together, we laughed and told jokes. And, if you asked, he would give you his last dollar. And, if you new how to get on his "good" side he would give you the shirt off his back. Always popular with the girls in school he was a "good" dresser, "great" dancer, and got "good' grades.

I can remember when we were in the 6th grade; my brother was a little chubby. Our school, Harbor Christian, held a sponsorship marathon and for every lap you ran they paid a dollar or more. Julius ran 30 laps. Because he felt he could have done better, he dropped weight over the next three months. From that point forward he remained trim. The personal drive he applied to losing weight, at 12, was a "good' quality he maintained in every endeavor for the rest of his life.

Julius was also "bad"!

"Fighter" should have been my brother's middle name. He never avoided a confrontation. He never let an insult pass. That's what made him "bad"!

Mom described him as "smellin' himself". That's how other people explained 13 going on 30. Julius was always in a rush to grow up. The same impatience he showed with time he showed with earning money.

We believed he could smell money a mile away. He smelled the change on my father's bureau. When he left the house, so did my father's change. That was the humble beginning of a "good" guy turning "bad".

And. with each "bad" deed, Julius would turn the rheostat up to a "worse" level.

Since he was my brother, I would always be right there, soaring to higher heights and lower lows.

Every year it would be something new, Swap Meets in '76; Dodger Stadium in '78, Kinney Shoes in '80.

After we started working at Dodger Stadium selling Coke and ice cream bars, the money we made wasn't enough for Julius. That's when he started the "vendors" dice game.

As a natural leader, others, including me, followed him for good or bad. Because he was confident, he generated confidence in others. This venture led to his first Camaro. Yes, my 16 year-old brother drove us down the path to iniquity in a sweet Camaro. In those years our end zone was Venice Beach. In the 80's that was the "hustlers" incubator.

The "ugly" was how he lost his life. We'll talk about that later.

8. Teachers & Talkers

Wherefore, my beloved brethren, let every man be swift to hear, slow to speak, slow to wrath: for the wrath of man worketh not the righteousness of God. Wherefore lay apart all filthiness and superfluity of naughtiness, and receive with meakness the engrafted word, which is able to save souls. But be ye doers of the word, and not hearers only, deceiving your own selves. For if any be a hearer of the word, and not a doer, he is like unto a man beholding his natural face in a glass (James 1:19-23). Anybody can talk the talk, but the real question is are you walking the walk. Guys when that beautiful young lady tells you it's on and crackin', or girls, the guys you always wanted, step to you, are you going to represent the kingdom of God or represent yourself. Those moments of pleasure can cost you big time. Those moments can cost you your life, your blessing or anointing,

To those of you who are in business of handling money, is it really worth it, running off with that money? Scripture tells us, *"what does it profit a man to gain the world and lose his soul."* That's just a temporary fix. Its not worth it. Now you have to lie to the business associates or to whomever you report. You can fool man, but you can't fool God! God's angels are taking record of everything you've ever done, like a CD or DVD, when you go before the Lord in judgment, He will be able to rewind the tape. Yes, you Will be on the big screen, God has a record of your life. But when we submit our lives to God, He takes our sins and throw them into a lake of forgiveness, He blots them out and doesn't remember them.

God says if you take one step I will take two. So beloved are you a teacher or a talker? Are you living the life or living a lie? Who's fooling who? It's not worth it. I'd rather be a door keeper in heaven, than lose my life to hypocrisy. Beloved, we are going to be rewarded or judged, that depends on us, as to how we are living this life. The best testimony is to live the life of a believer in your every day actions, that's a teacher who does not give in to sin, resisting the devil and temptation. The Bible tells us to yield not to temptation, but resist the devil and he will flee.

When someone calls you and leaves you a voice message or text, and you don't return their call, and in your spirit you know you should, remember, someone is always watching you and they look up to you. The way you carry yourself, impacts the way they carry themselves. Whether you like it or not, they are modeling themselves after you. We are responsible for imparting certain things into people's lives.

Phillip was assigned to the eunuch (ACTS 8:26-31). He was responsible for imparting certain knowledge, into his life. Just as Elijah gave Elisha a double portion, 2 KINGS 2:9-10, and

Samuel anointed David to be King, so are we anointed to take someone to the next level. God can come down himself and do it, but trust me beloved, you would be so overwhelmed that you wouldn't be able to handle it. So, therefore, He uses us to get the work done, and provides us an opportunity to earn Kingdom rewards. There are individuals that come into our life, and God expects us to pour into them. Sometimes it could be showing love, giving them money, a place to stay, shelter, a word from the Lord, just being a friend, a job or a connection.

Let God use you for the glory of the Kingdom. Lead by example. The example you make, will have a ripple effect. Sometimes we can touch one, and that one becomes thousands, then millions. Look at Dr. Martin Luther King, Jr. and his I have a dream speech, just by him having a dream, he moved millions of hearts towards a vision to be one world that doesn't discriminate because of race, color, gender or background.

I once heard Jesse Duplantis say, "Its not the poorest man that doesn't have a nickel in his pocket, it's the one without a dream. I challenge you today, to dream and dream big. Scripture tells us, a man without a dream shall perish, which makes all the sense in the world. If you are not living your dream, what are you living for? Joseph had a dream that he was ruler over many, including his brothers. He tried to give birth to the dream too early. With our dreams, let us also pray for discernment as to when to share them and with whom to share them, because there are also dream killers — those who seek out to abort your dreams.

May we stay in tune with the Holy Spirit, because the Holy Spirit will let you know just when to release your dream and to whom. Not everybody wants to see you succeed. There are demons individually assigned to you, to stop any and everything you want to do that is positive for the Kingdom of God.

However, there are angels fighting with you and for you. When Daniel fasted and prayed, his answered prayer was on the way by the angel, Gabriel. But Gabriel got held up by demons, and the angel, Michael, had to come and help him. So my friends put on the whole armor of God so you may be able to withstand the wiles of the devil. Stand up, and fight for your rights to be a fellow citizen of the Kingdom of heaven.

Recently someone very close to me invested $150,000 into an investment that is now at a stand still. They may or may not get a return. Only God knows. I have been approached with a $100,000 deal that seemed air tight, but the Spirit told me that something is just not right. Thank you God for discernment. It's awful that my close friend may lose $150,000. But in the mist of it, God uses that situation to let us know, that every deals that comes along that looks sweet, is not always sweet. Consider Job, God gave him double for his trouble. My friend my prayer for you is Divine intervention, that God intervenes and turn your situation around. There is no failure in God. Satan meant it for evil but God meant it for good. My friend, you might be facing a situation where you cannot see your way. But know that God can make a way out of no way. Stretch out your faith and believe God!

9. Laws, Rules and Principles

I BELIEVE GOD GIVES US LAWS TO KEEP US WITHIN THE boundaries of his commandments. When playing sports you are authorized to stay in certain boundaries, you step out of these boundaries you are penalized, it's the same with God's Kingdom, I recently saw an off-road race were a vehicle lost control and rolled over into the side lines, and innocent by-standers were badly injured. Also, in a bull fight, a bull jumped into the stands and again some people were badly injured.. That's the same when we are out of God's laws, we're subject to penalization.

Recently someone close to me was sentenced to numerous years, in the penitentiary, because they broke the laws of the United States Government. God also has laws and they aren't to be broken. Under any circumstances, His laws are laid down and laid out, end of story. And he will not go back on them under any means. I believe that God put His laws in place to protect and not harm us— it's for our safety. JEREMIAH 29:11 says, *"For I know the plans I have for you, plans to prosper you, to give you hope and a future, plans for good and not evil. Thou shall not covet thy neighbor's wife"*.

Think about it guys. If someone was looking at your wife in a lustful way, you're ready to confront them. God is stopping a bad situation before it even occurs. He's saying don't go down this road, because it's a dead end. Literally, many folks have lost their lives because they decided that they were going to travel down this lustful road, on forbidden ground — forbidden fruit. They decided to have an affair with someone's spouse. And it would ultimately cost them their lives. Speaking of forbidden fruit, God gave Adam in the beginning the garden which to attend. He told them you may eat any fruit of this garden, except this one tree, the knowledge of good and evil. If you eat of it, you shall surely die.

But one day in the garden, the serpent temped Eve and she gave in, she and Adam, and as the result of them breaking this law of God, we now have sin. That was not God's plan from the beginning, his plan was that we may live forever, with no lies, no cheating, no sickness, no sorrow, no death, that we would have life eternally.

Because a law was broken, things were changed. As long as we are here on this earth, but after we leave this earth, then there's the judgment, and then our eternal resting place. Whether it's heaven or hell, we will be judged according to our works. And I saw the dead, small and great, standing before God ; *"and the books were opened, which is the book of life; and the dead were judged out of those things which were written in the books, according to their works"* (REV 20:12). Dearly beloved, this is one of the major reasons that God's laws were put in place, that we may spend eternity, with our maker. The way to heaven is to walk in obedience to God's laws. If you break the laws of this earth, you will go to jail. If you break the laws of God, it's a good chance you will not go to heaven. God is merciful, but he is also just. God does forgive and he asks us to repent of all unrighteousness.

When Jesus, was on the cross there were two thieves, on each side of him. One believed in him and one did not. The one who believed in him, Jesus told him, *"This day shall you be with me in paradise"* (MATTHEW 27:38).

All things are possible to those who believe. Dearly beloved, if you just believe, that's the key. If you wanted to go through a door with a lock on it, you would need a key. Your key to God's Kingdom is belief in his Word. God says, *"those are mine who hear my voice and obey"* (JOHN 10:27). He says *"my sheep know my voice"*. God considers us as sheep, and he is concerned about each and everyone of us.

Read Matthew regarding the 99 sheep. God doesn't look at your race, color, gender or background. The will of God is that none shall perish. God wants us to have free will! To choose Him, or not, we don't have to choose God, but if we decide to go that route we forfeit all the benefits in believing God (DEU. 28:15). *"If you do not obey the Lord your God, and do not carefully follow all His commandments and decrees, I am giving you today, all these curses will come upon you and overtake you. You will be cursed in the city and cursed in the country, your basket and kneading through will be cursed, the fruit of your womb will be cursed, and the crops of your land and the calves of your herds and the lambs of your flocks. You will be cursed when you come in and when you go out"*. The Lord will send curses and confusion and rebuke in everything you put your hand to, until you are destroyed and come to sudden ruin, because of the evil you have done in forsaking Him.

May I submit to you this day beloved that your arms are too short to box with God. Look at the power of God in JOSHUA 6:20-21 and 2 KINGS 1:12, 19:32-35. *"Therefore thus saith the Lord concerning the king of Assyria, he shall not come into the city, nor shoot an arrow there, nor come before it with shield, nor cast a bank against it. By the way that he came, by the same shall he return, and shall not come into the city, saith the Lord. For I will defend the city. To save it. For my own sake, and for my servant David's sake. And it came to pass that night, that the angel of the Lord went out, and smote in the camp of the Assyrians a hundred fourscore and five thousand: and when they arose early in the morning, they were all dead corpses."*

10. Finding a Good Woman/Man

It should have ended "happily ever after." The groom was perfect. The bride was perfect. And, God blessed the union. But it failed miserably. We all know this story. Adam and Eve.

Genesis 2:18-24 reads:
"18 And God went on to say: "It is not good for the man to continue by himself. I am going to make a helper for him, as a complement of him." 19 Now God was forming from the ground every wild beast of the field and every flying creature of the heavens, and he began bringing them to the man to see what he would call each one; and whatever the man would call it, each living soul, that was its name. 20 So the man was calling the names of all the domestic animals and of the flying creatures of the heavens and of every wild beast of the field, but for man there was found no helper as a complement of him. 21 Hence God had a deep sleep fall upon the man and, while he was sleeping, he took one of his ribs and then closed up the flesh over its place. 22 And God proceeded to build the rib that he had taken

from the man into a woman and to bring her to the man. 23 Then the man said: "This is at last bone of my bones flesh of my flesh one will be called Woman from man this one was taken." 24 That is why a man will leave his father and his mother and he must stick to his wife and they must become one flesh."

If their perfect beginning failed, what will help a man and woman to succeed? Is there no hope?

If you think about it there is probably more written about love than almost any other subject. Good literature, bad literature, fiction and non-fiction you name it; and there is a hopeful love story. Romeo and Juliet, Anthony and Cleopatra, Samson and Delilah are all fabulous and memorable tales. Unfortunately, not one either fictional or historical love story turned out well. Nobody lived happily ever after. Is "true" love just a fantasy?

Many of us have been fooled. We have been led to believe that the Hollywood view of love is accurate. In most model stories boy-meets-girl, boy-loses-girl, boy-regains-girl. The formula works in CDs, books, and movies. But Hollywood's purpose is primarily to entertain, and not to educate. The highest grossing movies like Avatar, Titanic and Star Trek are blends of fantasy and romance made primarily to bring in the money. Sadly, though, for young and old alike, it is easy to confuse such fiction with reality.

We are left holding the bag. We are disappointed when our relationships do not match those of fictional characters on the screen or in the Romance novel. So how can we distinguish between fantasy and reality, between media romance and genuine love? The answer is not on the Internet.

Google "love" or "relationships" on the Internet and you have a flood of numerous web sites claiming to answer all your questions on how to find love. Some promise you "incredible secrets" from "match-making professionals," "relationship experts," and "love doctors". And, the claims are incredible. One of the most ridiculous claims states "in 90 minutes or less," you can find everlasting love.

Moreover, none of this "expert" knowledge is for free. The advice comes at a price. Most of us who fall for the "counsel" pay twice. First, the cost of the book or the seminar is readily offered in a variety of payment forms; second if the guidance turns out to be worthless, and it might, we pay an emotional tax when things don't work out as we expected.

Dr. Kevin Leman writes. "There's an ancient book that contains a description of love. The book is nearly two thousand years old, but it is still the best description of love I've ever read."

These words written by the Apostle Paul are found in the Greek Scriptures at 1 CORINTHIANS 13:4-8:

"Love is long-suffering and kind. Love is not jealous, it does not brag, does not get puffed up, does not behave indecently, does not look for its own interests, does not become provoked. It does not keep account of the injury. It does not rejoice over unrighteousness, but rejoices with the truth. It bears all things, believes all things, hopes all things, endures all things. Love never fails."

Most often used in marriage ceremonies, these words are not referring to "erotic" love between a man and a woman. Instead, they are describing "principled" love or **agape** love. the kind that describes God at 1 JOHN 4:8, *"...God is love."*

These words are simple and yet profound, and there is no clouding of truth. Unlike what exists on the Internet there are no wild promises or guaranteed claims. Though it was written long ago, this counsel is never outdated. No matter what our circumstances or background, these words teach us what we need to know about love. And its counsel is free.

Does this counsel guarantee "true" love? No, but it identifies the qualities we can expect *if* we find our own "true" love.

Is there a "soul" mate for each of us? The answer is unclear, since, each of us may have physical or emotional preferences. But, there is enough human variety to satisfy each and every one of us. Genuine love is by choice, and like faith, has a firm foundation.

Are you thinking about a relationship—either about a possible future marriage or about that relationship you are in now?

How do you know if you're really in love?

I started this chapter noting that Adam and Eve failed. And I mentioned that a real-life relationship is far different from that depicted in movies, on television, or in fictional romance novels.

But, a good relationship and future marriage of two mature people who are truly in love may be considered a blessing from God (Proverbs 18:22; 19:14).

But first, what if you are only attracted to losers?

I am one of those people. I believed everything the entertainment media sold me about an ideal woman. You name it, television programs, movies, and music videos all depicted the man I wanted to be for that ideal woman. Like the character Superfly, I tried to appear hard and cool. I was attracted most to women who appeared remote and self-centered.

This describes my first true love. With me, she was the opposite of Aretha Franklin's plea for R-E-S-P-E-C-T. Instead, her theme song should have been D-I-S-R-E-S-P-E-C-T. She took virtually every opportunity to abuse my affections. Between phone calls and home visits with "old" boyfriends, she batted my heart back and forth like a ping-pong ball.

I thought she must have hidden redeeming values like sensitivity and warmth. In my mind, I was that catalyst to turn this caterpillar into a beautiful butterfly. Yes, I thought I was the solution; just what she needed to bring these finer qualities to the surface. That's how television presents the story. It had me hook line and sinker. As you might guess, this romantic fantasy proved false in my "real" life. Sadly, I waited in vain for the butterfly—the selfish, toxic, willful caterpillar to appear but it never transformed into my perfect, sensitive soul mate. For example, we left church after hearing a dynamic message and hadn't even left the parking lot before she was cursing like a sailor. Those arguments increased over time. Eventually I realized that she loved chaos. I don't. You can imagine the conclusion. Bars, strip clubs and lap dances became my counteroffensive.

What I wanted was a positive relationship with an equal. What I got was more disrespect as she returned to her ex-boyfriend. I wasn't prepared for a relationship, let alone marriage.

Does that mean that true love does not exist? Where should any of us look to find the perfect match? eHarmony? Match.com? 24 Hour Fitness? Worship?

Let's keep it simple, a good woman/man is hard to find.

Can you imagine diving into the Pacific Ocean without first learning to swim? I'm from Compton. We are not known for swimming. Yet, I absolutely recognize such a foolish act is harmful—maybe even deadly. Think, about all the people who jump into marriage without a clue of how to deal with the responsibilities involved.

At LUKE 14:28, Jesus said, *"Who of you that wants to build a tower does not first sit down and calculate the expense, to see if he has enough to complete it?"* We must consider the costs. What is true of building a tower is also true of building a marriage.

Nobody expects to fail at marriage even though many of their relationships ended dreadfully. Oddly enough, one definition of mental illness is, "taking the same actions again and again, yet expecting a different result." There is no doubt most couples enter wedlock loving each other dearly. They expect to spend the rest of their lives together happily. Sadly, the dream of a happy marriage often proves to be just that—a dream. Upon waking up to reality, many have excuses or accusations or both.

WHY DO SO MANY MARRIAGES FAIL?

For the same reason that many business ventures fail. Bad preparation! With business though, money can often fix the problem or buy time leading to eventual success. But, most couples are not that patient, nor do they recognize the complexity of turning two independent souls into one flesh. There is no pill to take, and very few college courses can prepare young students for marital success.

Another force may be at work. Sometimes lust gets in the way.

You have probably heard when it comes to choosing a lover, "Follow your heart!" On the surface that sounds like great advice. It certainly is romantic. But, strong feelings may be involved.

Would you trust a compass placed near a magnet to point you to true north?

Where the heart's involved, making an honest assessment can be too difficult. Feelings (read lust) alone are not a reliable guide in the selection of a mate. Proverbs states: *"He that is trusting in* his own heart is stupid." Why? Because "the heart is more treacherous than anything else and is desperate" (JEREMIAH 17:9; NUMBER 15:39). To be treacherous is to be disloyal or traitorous. Would you trust a person who is known as a deceiver and a traitor? Our figurative heart can be devious. Clearly, a relationship is not necessarily good for us just because it feels right.

A Look at Ourselves and Our Mate

I like myself! I value me. But, I'm not sure what I deserve.
It's not brain surgery to figure out what you or I want in a mate. No doubt you can list the qualities your mate should have. It is much more difficult, to look at yourself to determine how you can contribute to a winning marriage. Self-scrutiny is vital, but often painful.

For example, ask yourself the following questions:

- Am I self-sacrificing?
- Am I past the "bloom of youth"?
- Am I committed to stay married forever?
- What makes me such a winner?
- What do I need to change about me?
- *Do I have the maturity needed to support a mate?*

King Solomon's words apply to married couples. *"Two are better than one,"* he wrote, *"for if one of them should fall, the other one can raise his partner up. But how will it be with just the one who falls when there is not another to raise him up?"*—ECCLESIASTES 4:9, 10.

More good advice comes from the apostle Paul who wrote, *"Clothe yourselves with the tender affections of compassion, kindness, lowliness of mind, mildness, and long-suffering*" (COLOSSIANS 3:12). This counsel is appropriate for both those who are preparing for marriage as well as those who are already married.

Perhaps you are considering the ways you will change your future partner. You like most everything about them, but....

Stop! Yes, stop right now!

The fact is, you become like your partner. My friend who has been married 56 years explains, " I was overly optimistic, and she was overly pessimistic. We both benefited, we are now both pragmatic and it works smoothly."

Understand, those with whom we spend our time exert great power and influence over us.

PROVERBS 13:20 emphasizes that this power can be for good or for bad:

"He that is walking with wise persons will become wise, but he that is having dealings with the stupid ones will fare badly."

A bride and groom, like two people riding in the same Chevy, inevitably head in the same direction and arrive at the same destination at the same time in the same condition. So ask yourself: 'Does the path we are now on lead to where I want to go? Will it take us closer to our emotional, material, and spiritual goals?'

So, I don't trust my feelings as my sole guide. It's good to get wise counsel.

The most reliable guide is God's Word. Unlike my or your imperfect heart, Bible principles will never betray us or let us down. How can Bible principles help us to find someone? And how can we avoid making a terrible choice in—a marriage mate?

A Good Look at Your Mate

Tired of looking in the mirror?

Proverbs 14:15 states, *"The shrewd one considers his steps."* This should be especially true when selecting a marriage mate. Yet, it has been rumored that many people spend more time choosing paint for a bedroom wall than investigating which person to marry.

What questions did my first love have the right to ask about me? Try some of these on.

- What kind of reputation do you have?
- Do you want children?
- What are your spiritual goals?
- May I meet your family?
- When do you want to meet my family?
- What are your views on marriage?

"Let there be no doubt, marriage is a divine institution. It was authorized and established by God" (Genesis 2:22-24). God designed the marital arrangement creating a permanent bond between a man and a woman so that they might complement one another. Love can be a perfect bond of union. As Amy's Girl points out, "Love is Glue!"

My first love and I had a major hurdle in our relationship and we could not overcome it.

We had poor communication skills.

Observers of human behavior report that women are seduced through their ears and men are seduced through their eyes. Whether this is inherent or learned Eve according to the Bible record was completely deceived. At Genesis 3:13, Eve said to God: "*The serpent—it **deceived** me and so I ate.*" The serpent used the spoken word.

Maybe if she and her divinely created husband Adam had communicated better, our circumstances today may have worked out very different.

But, they had poor communication. It was Adam who distanced himself from Eve after their sin by passing the blame to, "*The woman whom you gave to be with me, she gave me fruit and so I ate*" (Genesis 3:13).

So, what does good communication look like?

The Apostle Paul defined good communication as,"*...an interchange of encouragement.*"

Although, we usually think of verbal communications, it includes writing and signs. After all, God uses the written Word to communicate with us today. Implicit in its meaning is the sharing of ideas and sentiments. When it is positive, it makes you feel better. Why? It includes thoughts that are up building, refreshing, virtuous, praiseworthy, and consoling (Ephesians 4:29-32). Nevertheless, without trust and mutual respect for the other person, all communication becomes an exhalation.

In a good relationship or successful marriage Proverb 17:17 should find its purest translation: "A true companion is loving all the time, and is a brother/sister that is born for when there is distress."

WHAT STANDARD DOES THE BIBLE SET FOR A CAPABLE WIFE?

Three thousand years ago, in PROVERBS 31ST, Lemuel wrote a beautiful description of a capable wife. Today we might call her "super mom". Lemuel described a woman who took care of her family, traded with merchants in the marketplace, and acted as a realtor, tailor, and gardener.

How did her husband and family react? She was cherished. *"Her children call her blessed, and her husband praises her...She is worth far more than corals."*

Finding a good mate with whom to share life's joys and sorrows is truly God's blessing. It fills a void caused by loneliness or despair. It can satisfy our inborn craving for love, companionship, and intimacy.

God provided, *"I am going to make a helper for him, as a complement of him"* (GENESIS 2:18).

Thank God!

The apostle Paul wrote that those who marry will have *"tribulation in their flesh"*— is this true?

Any of us who have loved and lost, know these words are absolutely true.

The love-at-first-sight notion got me into trouble. I blame Adam.

My first love made me feel good. The first time I looked at her it took my breath away. Remember those romantic myths I mentioned earlier. Well I got blind-sided by the notion that love–at-first-sight is true.

What's wrong with this notion? A good relationship takes time. Good communication is never automatic. Expecting to "bond" without effort or knowledge is sheer foolishness.

True love is more than a glance, more than just a feeling. And, to work, it must be founded on common principles and common values. I mistook infatuation for love. That will always lead to disappointment.

Choosing a suitable mate requires more than a strong first impression influenced by lust or infatuation. So take your time. Research has shown that your love relationship affects every other function in your world.

Take your time and get it right.

Boy loses girl: An evil count kidnaps the beautiful woman and flees the castle. The prince embarks on a dangerous quest to find her. A spokeswoman for Romance Writers of America notes: "The main plot of the romance must concern two people falling in love and struggling to make the relationship work." In most novels the relationship *will* work—readers know that. Obstacles, often of an external kind, are overcome.

In real life there are usually problems of an external kind and of an internal kind. They may involve money, work, relatives, and friends. Problems also emerge when one person does not meet the other's expectations. In fictional characters, flaws are usually minor, but this is not always the case in real life. Further, real love does not carry us effortlessly through trials or differences in views, backgrounds, desires, and personalities. Rather, love involves cooperation, humility, mildness, patience, and long-suffering—qualities that do not always come naturally or easily (1 CORINTHIANS 13:4-7).

Boy gets girl: The prince rescues the beautiful woman and banishes the count. The couple marry and live happily ever after. An editor of romance novels advises would-be writers: "You need that happily-ever-after ending.... The reader should be satisfied that the couple is together and happy." Romance novels rarely portray their characters after years of marriage. During that time disagreements and a host of other challenges and difficulties may have tested the relationship. As divorce statistics show, in time many marriages fail the test.

"WHAT is the matter with him? He should know better," remarks an observer. Shaking his head in disbelief, another walks away muttering, "If he had a little common sense, he would never have done that." Have you perhaps heard similar comments? What, though, is "common sense"?

The word "sense" is defined as "accurate appreciation," "understanding," and "practical wisdom or judgment." It implies that a person has the ability to judge and decide with intelligence. Common sense evidently requires that we use thinking ability. Many people would rather let others do their thinking for them. They allow the media, their peers, or popular opinion to make decisions for them.

Common sense seems to be so lacking in today's world that an observant man once noted, "Common sense, in truth, is very uncommon." How can we acquire common sense? What are its benefits?

How Acquired?

A wealth of sound advice is found in the Bible

While it takes time, sustained thought, and consistent effort to develop good sense and fine judgment, common sense is certainly attainable. Consider three factors that can help us to acquire common sense.

Study the Bible, and follow its advice. The Bible, written in the finest language and with clear logic, is an excellent aid in gaining wisdom and good sense (EPHESIANS 1:8). For example, the apostle Paul admonishes fellow Christians: *"Whatever things are true, whatever things are of serious concern, whatever things are righ-*

teous, whatever things are chaste, whatever things are lovable, whatever things are well spoken of, whatever virtue there is and whatever praiseworthy thing there is, continue considering these things" (PHILIPPIANS 4:8). If we consistently follow this advice, sound judgment and prudent behavior will result.

Learn from experience. Associating common sense with experience in life, a Swiss poet stated: "Common sense is...composed of experience and prevision [foresight]." Indeed, *"anyone inexperienced puts faith in every word, but the shrewd one considers his steps"* (PROVERBS 14:15). Common sense may be developed through observation, training, and experience. We can learn to do things better over a period of time. Learning from our mistakes, however, calls for humility and meekness. The self-assuming, haughty, and headstrong spirit of people in these last days is not a manifestation of common sense.—2 TIMOTHY 3:1-5.

Common sense may be acquired through observation, training, and experience

Choose associates wisely. In using wisdom and common sense, we are also helped or hindered by our associates. PROVERBS 13:20 states: *"He that is walking with wise persons will become wise, but he that is having dealings with the stupid ones will fare badly."* We do not have to accept the mentality or ideas of those who disobey God and ignore his Word. PROVERBS 17:12 puts the matter this way: *"Let there be an encountering by a man of a bear bereaved of its cubs rather than anyone stupid in his foolishness."*

11. Hustlers & Gladiators

LET'S EAT, DRINK, AND BE MERRY FOR TOMORROW WE MUST die! That is the mind set of a hustler and gladiator. It's by whatever means necessary to accomplish their goal. Looking at the fight with Sugar Shane Mosley and Floyd Mayweather, you will see hustler and gladiator in both men. Both men held the key to a successful win. But one man was more confident than the other. Confidence and faith can be the key to your goal. If you sit and plan your goals you will see how far planning can take you. Their goal was to take each other out by whatever means necessary. Sugar Shane Mosley is very confident on the first two rounds but during the next eight rounds his performance declined. What happen? A friend of mind said "Mosley had been on a strict diet so that he could meet the required weight limit." The commentator said "He had just finish a fight, and was training hard but didn't give his body the proper time needed to rest, and maybe he shouldn't have been fighting."

When Mayweather first came out he didn't seem to be confident. But after the third round somehow gained a sense of who he was and began to deliver. Confidence is key! So a man thinks, that he is! If you think you'll win you will! And if you think you will lose, you will, it's inevitable. After producing for at lease nine rounds, Mayweather won the fight. And the commentator asked Sugar Shane Mosley, what happened and will he fight again. He said, that he had to go home rest up, look at the tape and take it from there. that's the thing about being a hustler/gladiator, you know that one mistake can cost you big! When one goes out to battle, he needs a well-mapped-out plan.

When Ali went against Foreman, he had a planned strategy, His plan was to hang on the ropes and tire Foreman out. The question was could his body stand the pounding, yes! He had it pretty much mapped out and it worked. He took all Foreman had, and then he said, "I'm going to give it to you." After taking a brutal beating from Foreman and wearing him out, Ali got explosive and gave Foreman all that he had for a TKO. My friend what's your plan? Are you going to do battle? You need to have a plan in place. Prayer is one of the most effective tools of warfare, whether we are talking spiritual of physical. You have angels acting on your behalf. Sometimes we have near death experiences and come out alive because of the prayers our families have been sending up. You thought it was just luck! No, it wasn't luck. It was the result of prayers.

In the movie 300, there's one part of the movie when the Persians tell the Greeks to put down their weapons, and the Greeks response is, come and get them. The Greek was heartless, ruthless, and relentless. They were on a mission that was unstoppable, like a train, this locomotive is coming through so you need to back up! That's the mind set we are talking about. This reminds me of Gideon's 300, those warriors had God on their side? Yes! When your purpose serves the Kingdom of God you are bound to win the battle. Although there were 300 Spartans present at the defense of Thermopylae, there were at lease 4000 allies involved on the first two days, and 1500 men involved in the fatal last stand. Still a tiny figure compared to the forces against them. Contributors forget more than the legend, the Persians army did in deed arrive at Thermopylae, and after their offer of free passage to the Greek the defenders were refused, they attacked on the fifth day, For forty eight hours the defenders of Thermopylae held out, defeating not just the poorly trained levies sent to dull them, but the immortals the Persians elite.

The Spartans, a brutal people with arguably the most militarize culture in history, could only reach manhood once they killed a slave. They agreed to defend Thermopylae. However, those grounds were given in 480 BC. Their enemy had to bring it! Because the Greek's Spartan 300 were well at strategizing in battle, highly skilled warriors, you weren't just going to be able to run up! They would train for battle everyday from a child to adult. By the time they were 18, they could have 14 years of training under their belt. Those 300 elite warriors would run through a large number of men, before it was all over. The Persians tried to take them out by bow and arrow. They were to strong. Strength is a key factor in battle, ISAIAH 40:31.

Let's take a look at the man of God in battle, see how God moves in battle, JUDGES 6:12. *"And the angel of the Lord appeared to him, and said to him, "The Lord is with you, you mighty man of valor!"*

JUDGES 6:25-30 36-40 "*And it came to pass that same night,that the lord said unto him, take thy fathers bullock, even the second bullock of seven years old, and throw down the altar of Baal that thy father hath, and cut down the grove that is by it: and build an altar unto the Lord thy God upon the top of the rock, in the ordered place, and take the second bullock and offer a burnt sacrifice with the wood of grove which thou shalt cut down. Then Gideon took ten men of his servants, and did as the Lord said unto him: and so it was, because he feared his fathers household, and the men of the city, that he could not do it by day, that he did it by night. And when the men of the city arose early in the morning, behold the altar of Baal was cast down, and the grove was cast down that was by it, and the second bullock was offered upon the altar that was built. And they said one to another, who hath done this thing? And when they inquired and asked, they said, Gideon the son of Joash hath done this thing. Then the men of the city said unto Joash, Bring out thy son, that he may die:... And Gideon said unto God, If thou wilt save Israel by mine hand, as thou hast said, behold, I will put a fleece of wool in the floor; and if the dew be on the fleece only, and it be dry upon all the earth besides, then shall I know that thou wilt save Israel by mine hand, as thou hast said. And it was so: for he rose up early on the morrow, and thrust the fleece together, and wringed the dew out of the fleece, a bowl full of water. And Gideon said unto God, Let not thine anger be hot against me, and I will speak but this once: let me prove, I pray thee, but this once with the fleece; let it now be dry only upon the fleece, and upon all the ground let there be dew. And God did so that night: for it was dry upon the fleece only, and there was dew on the ground.*" America and Nations around the world take a good look at this because this still applies today. I am talking about Israel. It's not a good idea to go against Israel. The percussion is going be incomprehensible, you watch, you wait, you'll see! JUDGES 7:14-25.

I was in the NJROTC and Law enforcement in high school, What happened to me that I made wrong turn, wrong choice? I saw my big brother driving the big fancy cars and wearing the fancy clothes, having all the ladies, and I wanted a piece of the action. That decision would cost me big time. Beloved my question to you is, Is it really worth it? I don't think so. I have been there, and done that, and no it's not worth all the fame and fortune. Solomon the richest man that ever lived, he had the best of everything, 700 wives, 300 concubines, castles with gold all through them, he calls it all vanity. God has created us with a desire that He and He only can fill. I had just about anything I could desire, yet there was something missing, That something was God. Beloved, my Mom would always say it's lonely at the top. Are you having, in your peak moments, friends that love you for you or love you for what you have. Is your walk in alignment with the Word of God! Or, are you just living a lie?

Judges 8:10, 8:22-23

Without faith it's impossible to please God! If you're reading this and don't believe, God cannot move in your life. Believing God cause men to triumph! As you notice, he went from 32,000 men to 10,000 to 300 why? God's looking for people that will trust and believe Him, regardless, and no matter what. Though He slay, yet will I trust Him. Beloved, once you fully trust Him. He's going to show up and show out!

I knew something was fishy when Rick moved next door to the spot. That would be the beginning of something interesting to come. Rick would always say be nice, be nice, yes he and my brother were being nice alright! I believe that Rick was at the spot for various different reasons. To watch over us, to keep the clientèle going and he would make more money at the spot. How many of you know that verse "The boyz in hood always hard, you come talking trash they'll pull your card." Unfortunately that's just what happened, the guys in the crew didn't get along too well, with the guys in my brother's crew. They argued about everything. So one day they called my brother, he and his buddy came over, and turned the spot out. They jump on the guys. I mean they were all over them like a pack of wolves. They let off about fifty rounds into their VWs. Now normally this wouldn't fly, we wouldn't go for that—no way. Because it was my brother it put me in an awkward position. So we just chilled. We weren't that money hungry that we would kill each other. So I looked at my brother and he looked at me, we were both pissed, both consumed with greed, but yet we still kept our sanity.

Growing up in the hood, having wisdom went a long way. It could mean life or death, or not going to prison for something stupid that you could have avoided or walked away from. It's been many times when guys challenged me. Oh yes, they wanted to box, but I would rethink the whole thing. Box for what? Just to prove I'm bad; just showing off in front of some people. It's like no! It's not worth it, to be sitting in the penitentiary over something you could have avoided. It's not because you are scared, but you are smart not to be fighting over stupid stuff. My friend, time is valuable and it's something you can't get back. Use your time wisely. So, my brother showed him and his guys that showing off would cost us big time! This happened before noon. Later, that evening, I had a feeling something would happen. Bad boy, bad boy, what you gonna do when they come for you! The crew was just chilling making money as usual nice little clientèle flowing. We were eating pizza and watching videos. It probably was ten of us all together, because we had some ladies over.

Everybody was upstairs I was downstairs talking to a lady friend, and all of a sudden I hear keys dangling, I knew right away what that was. Quickly I went to lock the bar gate, and Rick had a cord running from the garage to his apt, it stopped me from locking the bar gate. We were pretty much screwed. All of sudden, this lady police office was right there in my face, "get down!" "Get down!" Guns drawn. Boy I wondered what she had. I was thinking give me some of it! She had a serious adrenaline rush. She was hyped. Mama didn't take no mess, she was hyped big time and, super aggressive. She had her gun pent to me, it stuck to me like glue. The rest of the crew rushed upstairs. All you could hear was get down! get down! And a bunch of yelling. I know the crew was shocked. One of the guys, I believe, went to flush the products. After they had searched us, searched the place, and tore up the toilet, looking for products, they hauled us off to jail.

I paid bail for everybody. We got out. However, it was business as usual. We took more precautions this time, but yet and still they came back again. But this time no one was there, so we thought it's time to breakdown and rebuild. So we closed down shop and reset up at a new location. It was more east side Compton. We had to rebuild our clientèle, but that didn't take long. So, we threw a party at the new spot. My girl was incredible, in every aspect, looking mighty fly! Hey, you know what was on my mind. What the song says, "I got love on my mind!" My girl was very supportive. I believe I couldn't have had a better girl, at the time. She made it that much easier for me to handle my business, never really going against the grain, but she went with the flow. She was not a push over, but she knew how to carry herself well. She represented us in a worthy manner.

Everybody had a blast that night at the party. But in that game it's always business as usual. The very next day, it was back to business. In that game, it really mattered a lot to have someone in your corner. It could literally mean life or death. The last thing you needed was someone that's always challenging you. After all, you have plenty to contend with, such as the Police trying to catch you, robbers just waiting on you to slip, so they can come in like vultures.

So the spot would go well for a good while, until we made a fall. We took a big loss and it would set us back a great deal. We lost crew members, we took a break. Later my brother said, "Come work with me." I was shocked, but that was a deal you couldn't refuse. Oh boy was in the money. At times, he was making large amounts daily, each day was different, some were real good , and some were okay. So I was chillin' with my brother and friends. He was talking about buying ten birds. I was thinking, did I hear that right? I'm like, is he serious, and he's telling everybody. I'm going to let Kenny take my place.

My brother had to do 90 days in the County Jail, and that's where he met his assailant. When they met, he told my brother that he was a jacker and a killer. That's how that game is, they tell you that, but you think, hey, I been rolling the dice so, why should I stop now! I might take a hallow point to the dome, but right now I have to get this paper. So here I am at my brother's spot, took a fall, working on making a comeback. So it's 7:00 am, Friday, December 13,1985. My brother comes by in his car. I'm looking out the window and he puts on this big Kool-aid smile! And I'm like Cool! So I did not hear from him anymore that day. Later that day, I call my lady, "Hey let's hook up later." I'm thinking booty call, and it's all good. Meanwhile, my brother and his crew, have a dispute over the phone with my brother's killer. So my brother was thinking just like me, "booty call," because he had hooked up with this young lady. So my brother, being who he always was argumentative, and a fighter, goes over the guys house, he and the young lady, to settle the dispute that they had earlier. So when he gets to the guy's house, maybe one of his guys came out and put a gun to my brother's head, and took him and the girl in the house and tie them up. He tells my brother that he wants $100,000 in exchange for his and the girl's life. My brother asked him, "Why are you doing this?" He said, "I told you that I was a jacker & a killer." My brother told him, "You can run, but you can't hide." So, they called my brother's crew and told them that we have Julius and they want $100,000 in exchange for his and the girl's life.

So, Rick ended up showing up. Meanwhile, I got my girl to respond to the booty call and we went to my brother's spot and chilled, this is a really nice apartment, meant just for the crew. It's about 8:00 pm and one of the crew members let us in, but told us nothing about what's going on! So we went to the back room and chilled, watching some TV and talking, and thinking maybe I'm going to get lucky! Yeah, I got lucky alright!

So my girl is acting funny. There wasn't anything happening. You know ladies. They have that discernment; they can smell a rat ten miles away. Next thing you know, there was a big boom. The crew member that let us in jumped out the window. So it was my brother, the lady that was with my brother Rick and the jackers. They made the girl go to the back room, and they come to me and my girl's room. My brother says "Hey, that's my brother, because he had HK47 pointed at my stomach. They put us at gun point and have us to go to the living room. So now, the jacker and my brother are going in circles. He is saying "Where's the money at?" My brother's saying, "There is no money."

So the jackers were rumbling all through the apartment looking for the money and finally they found it. The next thing you know, you hear this big boom. It was gun shots. My brother and Rick were both shot in the chest, as the jackers ran off. I looked at my brother and Rick, they were both lying on the floor dying! Devastated, I told my girl to call an ambulance. We were like chickens with their heads cut off. It was unbelievable, but yet real.

So I told my girl, "Stay here with them. I'm going to the phone booth to call my parents, and tell them what happened." My mom answered the phone and I told her Julius just got shot. She says, "OK, we will be right there." At this point, it's probably 1:00 am in the morning, so I called my girl back and she told me that my brother had passed. That just sucked all the life out of my body. My older brother dead at 23. All the fun we shared would just be a memory all the good times all the great times.

To put the whip cream on top, at that time like days later, this song comes out Sunday, Monday, Tuesday, Wednesday, Thursday, Friday, life goes on, it with never be the same! So Rick lives maybe an hour after being shot in the chest, they took him to the nearby hospital. My brother died right there on the spot. So here we are, me, my parents, family and friends outside the apartment, waiting for the detectives to finish up inside. At this point, it's probably 9:00 am the next day. So, they finished up and brought out my brother in this body bag, that was so devastating to say the least!

It was like someone taking a sword a thrusting you threw with it! It was like a nightmare that would never end, you just wish you could wake up and say, "Oh. that's a bad dream." From that point on, my whole life would change. I would lose my brother, and maybe a year later, the girl I cared so much about, our relationship would end. Even though we would separate, it was a good separation. I would change my way of thinking. At my brother's and Rick's home going, about 30 young people would give there lives to God! Praise God! My brother and Rick would have loved that! All things work to the good of those who love him, and are called according to his purpose!

12. Full Circle

RAISE A CHILD IN THE WAY IT SHOULD GO AND WHEN IT GROWS old it shall not depart from it. Coming up as a kid, not going to church was totally out of the question—that was not an option. Papa and Mama didn't take any mess. Every Sunday, it was Sunday school, regular service, and evening service. Many of times, we had to go to three services on Sunday. Sometimes we would have a revival and that would last all week. Sunday-Friday we had musicals, plays, BTU meeting, usher board meeting, play rehearsals, National Baptist Convention. It was a lot, but it did my brother and I a lot of good. We knew Jesus, and Jesus' way of doing things. So the seed was planted.

Once you have watered it, make sure it gets the right amount of sun light, make sure it's in good soil, good ground, and then you will reap the harvest. Same with us we have to plant and trust God. Who's report are we going to believe? I chose to believe the report of the Lord. Even though things might not appear that the Lord is moving on your behalf, trust me beloved He is. We had so much church, that we needed to take a break. Give no room to the devil. Resist the devil and he will flee. We stop going to church, and did not set foot in church for years. Thank God we remembered all the principles.

My brother met my mother the Sunday before he was killed. He told my mother that it was well with his soul, meaning God is with me! They met for communion at the late great E.V. Hill church, MT Zion in Los Angeles, California. On Friday December 13,1985, at 12:00 am, he was killed. When we went to see his body, he had this great big smile on his face as through a angel had carried him off. Later I had asked God about my brother. That same night when I went to sleep, God showed him to me. My beloved brother. I had never seen him look so good. Everything was of perfection, like himself but everything was better. He had a perfect radiant smile. Skin perfect—everything perfect. In JAMES 1:4, the Word tells us that the will of God is for us to be perfect and complete and lacking nothing. Everything was unbelievably astonishing.

Beloved you can't beat God, no matter how hard you try. So being in the world nearly 15 years, I just got tired of the rat race, guys pulling guns on me visa versa, being shot at, all the manipulation, the hustle and bustle, the disappointments, the upsets, going around in circles, spinning my wheels. I said, "This is going nowhere fast." What profit a man to gain the world and lose his soul? It's not worth it. I rather have Jesus then silver or gold. So, my friends said to me let's go to Noel Jones'church—Greater Bethany, now known as the City of Refuge. I was burnt out from the world. Beloved, this is why I say to you, have your fun, don't be so spiritually minded that you are no earthly good. Too much of anything can be dangerous. Always put Christ first, but Christ doesn't want us to stop having fun, as long as it honors Him in what we do, go have fun, do what you like to do. Beloved, Christ came that we would have life and life more abundantly!

My girlfriend would always have some guys in my face, calling on the phone, dropping by old boyfriends, the whole nine yards. I got tired of being disrespected, so I started going to the bars, the clubs and getting lap dances. The girls would be like candy, wrapped up tight, real nice, good smelling perfume, vibrant. So this went on for about six months or maybe a year. I would take my cousin with me and my friends sometimes. We were having a ball, just like sex, but dry sex. At the same time, I was giving myself back to the Lord, at least thinking about it. I believe God said, "I'm tired of this mess." One night I went to bed and there it was, God showed me the spirit behind lust, it was awful, they looked like trolls, something out of a horror movie. In so many words, He said, this is what you're your dancing with! It didn't take long after that, I would go to church more and more.

We couldn't get enough of Noel Jones' dynamic preaching. I can remember one time he was preaching and he said, "because you're in Christ, your stock has went up!" Scripture tells us when we are in Christ we are qualified to share into his inheritance. It tells us that we are the head and not the tail, above and not beneath. It tells us forget not His benefits. For some reason, I was growing at a faster pace than my girl. When we would leave church, the preacher had preached a dynamic message, and all of a sudden before pulling out the church's parking lot an argument would break out. She would be cussing like a sailor. I said to myself, this has got to stop, there's no way that I'm going to get out of church, hear a dynamic message, and do not apply it to my life.

The arguments, the craziness, the chaos, had been going on probably two years off and on, so I knew something had to be done. I knew this was not the way that I was going to live my life. I told her that I wanted a relationship where I could hold and caress my mate. She just looked at me and smiled. For some reason she didn't want to let go of the chaos. So I decided to let it go slowly but surely. And at that time, to make matters worse, her old boyfriend showed up on the scene. There's a way that seems right to men but in the end there's destruction.

Introduced to environmental work

As I sought after God, the jobs just kept getting better and better. I imagine God said, "I'm going to get rid of your enemies little by little!" It was fun working for the security company; they had me all over Los Angeles. At one point, I was a rover, meaning that they would use me as a replacement, so I would fill in for the guys who were sick or on vacation. My checks were pretty good, because I would get lots of overtime. Finally I would get a post, at UPS and my job would be to sign the guys in as they pull in. They had a seal on the back of their trailer, and I would be the one to cut it off. Some guys would pull doubles, and triples meaning two and three trailers.

One day I met a friend and he introduced me to environmental work. I registered with the agency, went and got all my necessary certificates, the next thing for me, they were sending me out on jobs. It just kept getting better and better. It was a temp agency so the job would last anywhere from a day to a week to a month or even go permanent. God says in Psalms, forget not his benefits. So my Aunt and Mom would go to Hawaii for my cousin's job, and she invited my Mom and my Aunt, and Mom would invite me. Look what the Lord has done. So we all went and had a blast in Honolulu — an incredible time. We had so much fun. I didn't want to leave. We visited Pearl Harbor, the zoo, the mall, all over, and we would go to the beach and look at the water. It was crystal clear. When it was time to go back, I didn't want to leave.

So when we returned to LA it was business as usual, back to church, back to work. It had all began to balance out, not too much work, not too much church—perfect. Thank God this is what I'd been needing all along. This has kept me stable until this day.

The environmental agency asked me if I would travel, and I told them, "Yes". So I got the opportunity to go to Arizona to do some drilling at the military base. It was pretty exciting being on base. Being that I always wanted to go into the military, that was a great job. We drove up, and drove back; we probably stayed there maybe a week. The pay was decent and we would get per diem pay for personal hygiene, etc.

The same way you would go and hear a motivational speaker or talk with a counselor, that's the way the word of the Lord is from a minister, but better. It's the Word fresh from heaven, depending on how anointed your minister is and if you are tuned into the Holy Spirit, the more the better. You can be outside of God's kingdom and using His principles and be blessed, although I wouldn't recommend it.

So I would finally end that relationship, just to go into another one, not giving myself time to heal. I would start a relationship with a young lady from Belize, it was a better relationship in a lot of ways. But some of her morals were different from mine. She felt obligated to her family regardless, being that they were from Belize, and she was the oldest, she felt like she was suppose to take care of them, period. But I saw it differently. I told her that her relatives were past 21 and she had been taking care of them for a number of years, let them go. But she didn't see it that way. Some people are opportunist, if they see where they can get over on you they will. I didn't mind her looking out for them sometimes, but when it's time for the little birds to leave the nest, you have to let them get out there and experience life. How else are they going to grow? We could never see eye to eye. We were together maybe a year.

An opportunity came through for me to take a job in Sterlin, Colorado. Prior to getting the job I had prayed and asked God to send me to a distant land, and two weeks later, I get the call from the environmental company. I had been faithful in attending Noel Jones Church, didn't miss a beat. I was there faithfully every Sunday, and every Wednesday. Every now and then, he would speak out of town, and we would go and see him. My first love and I had a chance to see him speak in Palm Springs. Oh, what a beautiful occasion that was. We drove up that Friday night, spent the night at the resort, had breakfast, and went to hear Bishop Noel Jones speak. What a great day that was!

13 Finding the Truth

I WAS SPINNING MY WHEELS, JUST GOING AROUND IN CIRCLES, for years. I finally said I'm fed up with going nowhere. The drinking the getting high, the fights the arguments, the chaos, I ask myself the question, is this really worth it? Is this the way you want to spend the rest of your life? So, after being fed up, I was looking for a way out. I shared with my friend and she suggested that a friend of hers had found this great church around the corner, which was Greater Bethany, and the Pastor was Bishop Noel Jones. I said "what the heck? What do I have to lose?" My life right now is a mess, it's a wreck. Beloved, the same way you can be hooked on drugs, is the same way you can be hooked on God. It's a matter of desire. What's your desire? Being hooked on drugs are strongholds, which are from Satan. To be hooked on God is the anointing. It's a matter of choice. Do you choose to be up or down? It's up to you. Do you want the strongholds which are from Satan, or do you want the anointing which is from God (Deu. 28). Strongholds which produce dead works, or anointing which produces good fruit, Gal. 5:17. As soon as we went to that Church, the anointing of God hit us like bam!!!

One day I walked in high off drugs and alcohol, but when I walked out I was high off the Holy Spirit, praise God! The anointing will break every yoke of you; take every burden away. The word tells us to cast our cares on the Lord for He cares. Beloved, God takes our sins and throws them into a lake of forgiveness. He blots them out and remembers them no more. God is not mad at you, He loves you, and He only asks that you repent of all unrighteousness. So we would go every Sunday and every Wednesday, and didn't miss a beat. Just like that, we went from darkness to light. We did it and you can too. In only one day that's all it takes beloved. All you have to do is make that one step. You make one step, God will make two. The anointing will draw you. Satan is powerful but God is all powerful. When Job was tested, Satan had to get permission from God. You say if God loves us why does He allow things to happen to us? If we had not gone through anything, who could we win to Christ?

Everybody has been, or is going through something, but it's for our own good (Romans 8:28). No test, no testimony. I'm one who could tell you, what could have happened to me if God hadn't spanked my behind. Oh yeah. The same way you discipline your child, God disciplines you. Beloved, He chastens those ones he loves. If I had not run into a brick wall, my head would have been so puffed up, prideful, arrogant, it would take a crane to carry it around, and we have to go through the fire. It has been said in order to get gold to its finest form, you have to put it into the fire to get rid of all the impurities. God is getting all the impurities out of us, because He's coming back for a Church without spot or wrinkle. The Word says, *"Know that he that begins a good work in you shall perform it to the very end."* You might question that, I say to you don't. The Word tells us, lean not to your own understanding. The last thing you want to do is to figure out or question God. God tells us in His words; my thoughts are not your thoughts. Just as far is the heavens from the earth, my thoughts are further than yours.

14. My Truth

The fool hath said in his heart, There is no God. Corrupt are they, and have done abominable iniquity: there is none that doeth good. God looked down from heaven upon the children of men, to see if there were any that did understand, that did seek God. Every one of them is gone back: they are altogether become filthy; there is none that doeth good, no, not one. Have the workers of iniquity no knowledge? who eat up my people as they eat bread: they have not called upon God. There were they in great fear, where no fear was: for God hath scattered the bones of him that encampeth against thee: thou hast put them to shame, because God hath despised them. Oh that the salvation of Israel were come out of Zion! When God bringeth back the captivity of his people, Jacob shall rejoice, and Israel shall be glad.

"Save me, O God, by thy name, and judge me by thy strength. Hear my prayer, O God; give ear to the words of my mouth. For strangers are risen up against me, and oppressors seek after my soul: they have not set God before them. Behold, God is mine helper: the Lord is with them that uphold my soul. He shall reward evil unto mine enemies: cut them off in thy truth. I will freely sacrifice unto thee: I will praise thy name, O Lord; for it is good. For he hath delivered me out of all trouble: and mine eye hath seen his desire upon mine enemies." (PSALMS 53, 54).

One night in Los Angeles I decided to drive down an alley. This decision would nearly cost me my life. So I got halfway down the alley and some guys stop me, and the guys told me that I had just come through there earlier, and I shot at them. I told the guy "No I didn't." Then one of the guys put a double barrel shot gun to my forehead. And they said to me, "Yes you did." I'm shaking, thinking I'm getting ready to lose my life. I put my hands out the window to let the guys know that I did not have any firearms. Also there were guys in the building behind him hanging out the windows with guns pointed at me. So the guy and I go around in circles for at lease five minutes, he kept saying it was me, and I kept saying it wasn't me. So I thought this conversation is going nowhere. I might as well make a run for it, at lease I'll lose my life trying to save it! So, I just punched the pedal to the metal. Why did I do that? Those guys lit my mustang up. They let off more than enough rounds to do some damage! They lit my car up like Swiss cheese, bullet holes were everywhere. I don't know 'til this day why I wasn't hit!

So that encounter gave me what I needed to make the decision to try Jesus. *"This poor man cried, and the Lord heard him, and saved him out of all his troubles. The angel of the Lord encampeth round about them that fear Him, and delivereth them. O taste and see that the Lord is good: blessed is the man that trusteth in Him. O fear the Lord, ye His saints: for there is no want to them that fear Him. The young lions do* lack, and suffer hunger: but they who seek the Lord shall not want any good thing." (PSALMS 34:6-10).

If you lose your life you will save it, but if you try to save it you will lose it! The grass withers, the flower fades but the Word of the Lord is forever. Only what you do for Christ will last. It's not how much money you have made, Your CEO position at the Company, or how many bars and stripes you've earn in the military, or how much work you've put in on the streets. At the Day of Judgment, God is not going to ask you about your good deeds or good works. It's not by good works that any man should boast. You have to go that extra mile and except Jesus Christ as your Lord and savior. You say that you're a good person. Being a good person should make it that much easier to except Jesus Christ as your Lord and savior. On the Day of Judgment, God is going to ask you what you have done for the Kingdom. Work while it's still day because when night comes no man can work. When you're in Christ, to die is gain. This earth is beautiful, but heaven, beloved, is even more beautiful. Dearly beloved, there's only one way to the Kingdom of God and that's through Jesus Christ. Jesus said *"No man comes to the Father except by me."* 0 will you except Jesus Christ in your heart today? (JOHN 6:44-48)

Sinner's prayer! Dear God, as best as I know how, I give you my life. Jesus, forgive me of all my sins, I want to follow you. I ask you to come into my heart and be the Lord of my life. Take control of my life and I give myself to you. Thank you for hearing my prayer. I love you Lord. In Jesus name I pray, Amen. So, I encourage you to read your Bible and pray at lease once a day. Start off small and work your way up. Get connected to a good Church, and fellowship with other believers, forsaking not the assembly of one another. Yes, you can watch Church on the Internet or TV, but God's desire is for us to be whole, a man is not an island. It's the plan of the enemy Satan to have you alone for he can temp you. He is walking to and fro seeking whom ever he can destroy, Job 2:1-3. Two is better than one. If one should fall he has another to pick him up (Eccles. 4:9-10). I challenge you beloved today to connect with other believers. You notice when Jesus came to this earth, He chose twelve disciples. Why? Because the work that had to be done was not for one man to do alone. The harvest is plentiful, but the laborers are few. Jesus had to teach them the ways of the Lord. You can learn a lot from the Internet or TV, but a lot of things what're of God; you have to learn hands on. Me being a young minister coming up, a lot of things I have to ask my spiritual Fathers because I just don't know. I watch a lot of TBN, and Daystar, but it's just not enough if you want all God has for you.

Our assignment is the great commission, go ye into the entire world and preach the gospel. You can start with your family and friends, and move on from there. When I started going back to Church, I used to go sit in the pews. In Ecclesiastes, it tells us there's a time and a place for everything. But after sitting in the pews for awhile and learning all you can, it's time to get up and get active in the Church. Maybe your gift is a great smile, or a great personality. You can be an usher or a greeter, or a front desk secretary. If you like outdoors, security or parking lot ministry, and if you like traveling, evangelist or missionary. Wherefore He saith, when He ascended up on high, He led captivity captive, and gave gifts unto men. And He gave some apostles, and some prophets, and some evangelists and some pastors and teachers; for the perfecting of the saints, for the work of the ministry, for edifying of the body of Christ: Eph. 4:8, 11, 12. And if you like to counsel, do Prison ministry,

Outreach feeding the homeless and witnessing to them, looking after the widows and orphans, or become a Church Counselor. We the Church witness to our own which is in the will of God, but we also need to go outside the Church and witness. So you may be at Church every time the Church doors open, but I challenge you to go outside the Church and witness. At the grocery store, the laundromat-o-mat, cleaners, or the family reunion, Wal-Mart — somewhere outside the Church. The Holy Spirit will give you the discernment to know whom and where and when. Just ask Him, stretch out your faith and trust God.

15. Our Hope

Jeremiah 29:11 says, "for know the plans I have for you declares the Lord, plans to prosper you and not harm you, plans to give you a hope and a future." There you have it, God says in His Word that He has plans for us, good plans for a hope and a future, that's enough to start shouting and dancing right there.

In Numbers, it tells us that God cannot lie. And again in Titus 1:2 in hope of eternal life, which God that cannot lie, promised before the world began. These promises were made before the World began. Rev 3:20 says, *"Here I am standing at the door and knocking, if anyone hears my voice, and open the door, I will come in and eat with him, and he with me."* I feel like dancing!!! Don't you? It's wide open! It's up to us.

We plan our own destiny; we are Captains of our own ship. But I'll be the first to tell you that not having Jesus is like having a ship without a rudder. As the song writer says , "I'm lost without you." We can go without Jesus that's true. Have you ever seen a baby in his walker making his way and every now and then he bumps into something, and his parents have to step in and put him back on track, that's the same way with us believers.

We make our way okay but every now and then we have bumps that we need our parents to step in, Who might that be, none other than Jesus Christ himself. I must confess to you, God is more than enough of what you need, to succeed in this life. He will never leave you or forsake you. Will He put you through some test? Yes! Consider Job, he lost all that he had, but after he proved himself faithful to God, God gave him back double!!!! Behold happy is the man whom God correcteth: therefore despise not thou chastening of the almighty: for He maketh sore, and bindeth up: He woundeth and His hands make whole. He shall deliver thee in six troubles: yea in seven there shall be no evil touch thee. In famine, He shall redeem thee from death: and in war from power of the sword. Thou shall be hid from scourge of the tongue: neither shall thou be afraid of destruction when it comet. At destruction and famine thou shalt laugh: neither shalt thou be afraid of the beast of the earth (JOB5:17-27). And the Lord turned the captivity of Job, when he prayed for his friends: also the Lord gave Job twice as much as he had before (JOB 42:10).

REV. 22:12 says, *"And, behold, I come quickly; and my reward is with me, to give every man according as his work shall be."*

www.ingramcontent.com/pod-product-compliance
Lightning Source LLC
Chambersburg PA
CBHW020918090426
42736CB00008B/683